EARTH GOSPEL

---

*A Guide to
Prayer for God's
Creation*

Sam Hamilton-Poore

Illustrations by
Jane Wageman

UPPER
ROOM BOOKS®
NASHVILLE

MORE PRAISE FOR *EARTH GOSPEL*

I love this book! It is a gift to Christians (and others) who wish to praise the Creator through the creation. It is an exceptionally rich, varied collection of resources: prayers, scriptural passages, hymns, theological reflections, and poetry. I read it with delight, as it is full of eco-spirituality "gems" for both private and public worship.

—SALLIE MCFAGUE

Vancouver School of Theology, author of *A New Climate for Theology: God, the World, and Global Warming* and *Life Abundant: Rethinking Theology and Economy for a Planet in Peril*

All who are concerned about the care of the earth will cherish this prayer book by Sam Hamilton-Poore. This remarkably wide-ranging treasure trove of prayers, blessings, hymns, texts, and meditations will certainly be a valued resource for many in their individual and communal reflections regarding the earth.

—TERENCE E. FRETHEIM

Luther Seminary, author of *God and World in the Old Testament: A Relational Theology of Creation* and *The Suffering of God: An Old Testament Perspective*

In the seventh century, Maximus Confessor spoke of prayer as being intrinsically cosmic. Far from implying escape from this world, prayer involves kneeling on this earth as God's creation. This book reminds us that meditating on the heavenly kingdom cannot be disconnected from mending the natural environment.

—JOHN CHRYSSAVGIS

Ecological Advisor to Ecumenical Patriarch Bartholomew I of the Orthodox Church and author of *Light Through Darkness, Beyond the Shattered Image,* and *Soul Mending*

A prayer guide like no other. Sam Hamilton-Poore has done Christians a great service. Open your eyes, open your spirit; pray with this guide and you will see the world with new eyes!

—ELIZABETH LIEBERT

San Francisco Theological Seminary, author of *The Way of Discernment: Spiritual Practices for Decision Making* and *The Spiritual Exercises Reclaimed: Uncovering Liberating Possibilities for Women*

Spirited humans celebrate and care for the good Earth; and *Earth Gospel* leads the way. A splendid resource—or, better, a profound probing of the deepest sources of both nature and spirit. Here is healing for those anxious for a planet in jeopardy.

—HOLMES ROLSTON III

Colorado State University, 2003 Templeton Prize Laureate, and author of *Environmental Ethics: Values in and Duties to the Natural World* and *Genes, Genesis, and God*

EARTH GOSPEL
A Guide to Prayer for God's Creation
Copyright © 2008 by Sam Hamilton-Poore
All rights reserved.

UPPER ROOM®, UPPER ROOM BOOKS®, and design logos are trademarks owned by The Upper Room®, a ministry of GBOD®, Nashville, Tennessee. All rights reserved.

The Upper Room Web site: www.upperroom.org

Cover and interior design: Bruce Gore/Gorestudio   www.gorestudio.com
Cover photo: Shutterstock
First printing: 2008

ISBN: 978-0-8358-9943-7

♲ Printed in the United States of America on recycled paper.

Contents

ACKNOWLEDGMENTS

THE CREATION OF THIS PRAYER BOOK has been inspired by particular experiences I have shared with particular people who live near or along the banks of a particular river. Willow Creek in Mason City, Iowa, is a medium-sized river whose waters join with other streams that eventually flow into the Mississippi. A variety of oaks grows along the river's banks, with pockets of ancient prairie grasses and flowers. Depending upon the time of day and season of the year, you may see and hear deer, squirrels, rabbits, raccoons, muskrats, beavers, otters, migrating geese and grebes, great blue and green herons, hawks and owls, bald eagles, box and snapping turtles, dragonflies and damselflies. And there is always the river itself—in the winter, frozen and snow-buried; in the spring, surging with snowmelt; smooth flowing in the summer; and in the fall, a mirror of autumnal color.

During the years that my family and I lived in Mason City, Willow Creek became a favorite place for prayer and recreation. It's not so much that I went out to Willow Creek and then found a spot to pray; it's more accurate to say that every time I came within sight or sound of the river, I found myself in prayer. Wading into Willow Creek was like walking into a sanctuary where a divine liturgy was already in progress—a liturgy that the creation itself was singing to its Creator. I experienced myself and creation as "held" in the hands of Christ, the "first-born of all creation," who holds together all life, all creation. If the Holy Spirit—"the Lord, the giver of life" (Nicene Creed)—continually bears witness to the risen Christ and draws us into the life of Holy Trinity, then Willow Creek is a great and intimate friend of the Spirit. In my own mind, heart, imagination, and prayer, the great blue herons that fish the waters of Willow Creek are icons of the presence of the holy.

Also living and growing near the banks of Willow Creek are many people who participated in the making of *Earth Gospel*. They shared with me their love for God and God's creation. They prayed with me and for me in the writing of this prayer book and field-tested its first versions. Some of these people were also members of our church-based, monthly volunteer "Water Quality Monitoring Team" from First Presbyterian Church that—sunshine, rain, ice, or snow—entered knee-deep into the river to track its health. My deep thanks to all these dear friends: Susan Armstrong, Katherine Broman, Pat Dixon, Jack Gannett, Ken Gehling, Ken Hatland,

Joyce Hanes, Corita Heid, John and Judy Henry, Jim and Ann Kuhlman, Aaron Krogh, Kerry Dolch Krogh, Steve Krogh, Michael Lalor, Darrel Lind, Ann and John MacGregor, Sharon Magelssen, Yvonne Nutting, Robert Powell, Joel Rogers, Carol Shutte, Bob Towner, Jane Wageman (who also provided illustrations for *Earth Gospel*), and Craig Zoellner.

Any river is always part of a much larger hydrological cycle, with wide-ranging sources of water and life. Since *Earth Gospel* is also part of a much larger cycle of prayer, the circle of my gratitude widens to include Elizabeth Liebert, Deborah Arca Mooney, and Elizabeth Nordquist—my colleagues and friends in the Program in Christian Spirituality at San Francisco Theological Seminary. In particular, I thank Elizabeth Nordquist for the way in which she nurtured *Earth Gospel*. Much like the Holy Spirit in Hopkins' poem, Elizabeth "bent" and "brooded" over my manuscript with "warm breast" and "ah! bright wings." My thanks also to Terence Fretheim of Luther Theological Seminary, who vetted my Bible Comments, and to the kind, creative, and prayerful people at Upper Room Books: Rita Collett; Denise Duke; and my editor, Robin Pippin.

Lastly, I wish to thank the people who regularly give me most reason to praise our Maker. My parents, Billy and Ruthann Poore, nurtured me in the faith, set me free to play in the woods and creek near our home, and instilled in me a passion for the ocean. In our marriage and friendship, my wife, Terry, inspires me with faith, hope, love, creativity, honesty, beauty, and humor. And our children—Ben, Eliza, and Noah—bring us not only great joy but all the more reason to care for the present and future of God's creation. The circle of our family's love is also widened immeasurably by our animal companions, Sophie and Blackjack.

It is in gratitude to our Creator Spirit for her gift of my family that I dedicate *Earth Gospel* to Terry, Ben, Eliza, Noah, Sophie, and Blackjack.

I thank my God every time I remember you,
constantly praying with you in every one of my prayers for all of you,
because of your sharing in the gospel from the first day until now.
—*Philippians 1:3*

SEPTEMBER 1, 2008
DAY OF PRAYER FOR THE ENVIRONMENT
ORTHODOX CHURCH

INTRODUCTION

Why This Prayer Book? Why Now?

I OFFER THIS PRAYER BOOK TO CHRISTIANS who know or suspect that there is a direct connection between loving God and loving God's creation. I offer the prayer book as a guide for exploring—through a sustained period of prayer, meditation with scripture, and prayerful reflection—the interconnecting love that binds together God, humankind, and creation.

People from other faith traditions may use this prayer book, of course; but I have designed it with Christians in mind because in my life and work as a Presbyterian pastor, spiritual director, and environmental activist, I have met many Christians who assume that their own faith has little, if anything, to say about why or how followers of Jesus Christ should love or care for the creation. After all, doesn't the Christian faith call us to *reject* this world in favor of a world to come? Aren't we supposed to set our sights on heaven and forget the things—the birds, beasts, fields, and forests—that will sooner or later "pass away"? Any Christian who spends even a single morning with this prayer book will discover quite the opposite. The biblical texts, prayers, and readings in this prayer book summon Christians to embrace and care for God's creation with faith, hope, and love—not *in spite of* but precisely *because of* our relationship with the Spirit of God in Jesus Christ.

I also offer this prayer book because the creation that God loves is in a state of crisis as evidenced by such phenomena as global warming, soil erosion and desertification, air and water pollution, and a rapid extinction of species due to habitat destruction. This environmental crisis has emerged as a result of human activity, and its effects are experienced most profoundly among the poor.[1] Centuries ago, the apostle Paul wrote that creation is "groaning" and "waits with eager longing for the revealing of the children of God" (Rom. 8:19, 22). Paul's words speak with an even greater urgency in the twenty-first century. *For the creation today—and the human and nonhuman life it sustains—desperately needs Christians who will love and care for it with a love akin to that expressed by the Creator who sent the "only Son" to heal and restore the world* (John 3:16-17).

Christian love-in-action on behalf of the earth is essential, and there's no end to what needs doing: reducing human impact on the environment, lowering emissions of greenhouse gases, preserving or restoring ecosystems and habitats, and more. But I also believe that our action needs to include the "work" of Christian prayer, for prayer is a way of taking action. As John Calvin reminds us, prayer is the "chief exercise of faith" and a way "by which we daily receive God's benefits."[2] Prayer and action are not two separate matters for Christians; how we *live* is informed and shaped by how we pray and how we *pray* is informed and shaped by how we live. Furthermore, through prayer, we seek to align ourselves—heart, mind, soul, body, strength—with what *God* is doing in and through our lives, our communities, and the creation itself. Prayer energizes and inspires our love-in-action.

No matter the depth, breadth, or effectiveness of our action, even the most optimistic Christians may feel hopeless or incapacitated due to the immensity of the environmental crisis. This hopelessness or inertia is another reason Christians need to include prayer as a regular part of their care for the creation. In helping us stay consciously connected to God, prayer also helps us remain rooted in *hope*—hope for ourselves and hope for the creation. The God we encounter in prayer is a God of hope. Or to state it more directly, God *is* our hope; and God is trustworthy and gracious. Marjorie Thompson writes that our prayer itself expresses the hope that "God is continually working for good in the midst of ambiguous situations and that God's purposes will prevail in the end."[3] To become more attuned to God's presence is not only to ask for help but to ground ourselves—each time we pray—in God's own self, the source of our hope.

I trust that all who read and use this prayer book will rediscover the profound Christian witness—lyrical and long, biblical and beautiful—that the triune God loves this creation and is at work recreating and restoring it in and through the Spirit of Christ. May this rediscovery bring hope to more Christians and lead them to a renewal of prayer and action on behalf of God's beloved but groaning creation.

How to Use the Prayer Book

Structure of the Prayer Book and Options

Earth Gospel offers prayers for twenty-eight days (four weeks). Each day has three prayer settings: morning, midday, and evening; each day of the week has an identified theme (more about these themes below.)

The first way you may approach the prayer book, then, is according to its design. Begin with Week One: Monday; then work your way through the prayer book, day by day, week by week. You may engage in Morning Prayer anytime between waking and heading off to work, school, or other responsibilities. A lunch break or anytime during the day when you can set aside a few minutes may afford a time for Midday Prayer. Evening Prayer may take place at the end of the day, perhaps between the evening meal and sleep. There is room for flexibility. For example, one person who has used this prayer book discovered that Midday Prayer worked best after he arrived home from work rather than during his lunch break.

The length of time you devote to each prayer segment is also flexible. Some who have used this prayer book found that Morning Prayer required as little as ten to fifteen minutes. Others have chosen to take longer, lingering with the texts and expanding their time for meditation and prayer. You may find that no two days are exactly alike and that, depending on your responsibilities, you may have more time for prayer on one day than another. If you decide to devote a regular time each day to using the prayer book—say, for example, 7:30 AM for Morning Prayer—it is important that you find a balance between maintaining a daily discipline and being open to the peculiar rhythms of each particular day. Both *commitment* and *flexibility* will be important.

If you choose to begin at the beginning and move day by day and week by week to the end, then you will experience an immersion over time in the rich biblical witness to the relationship between the Creator and creation, as well as the church's witness to humankind's place within God's still unfolding grace. Other readers have benefited from using the resource this way, feeling as if they had engaged in a month-long retreat.

But you may use the prayer book in other ways. One of my first readers, an on-call nurse with a local hospice, found herself unable to set aside regular times for prayer. She might be called out during the middle of the night to assist a dying patient, which would leave her physically or emotionally depleted the next morning. So rather than trying to maintain a fixed schedule of prayer, she chose to leave the prayer book open on her kitchen countertop. Wherever she last left off in prayer, the book remained open, awaiting her return. She didn't care if she prayed Monday's prayers on Thursday or Midday Prayer at 2:00 AM. She found her own balance and rhythm between commitment and flexibility, and it worked well for her. I hope you will find your own balance.

Small groups may also use the prayer book. Each group member has a copy of the prayer book and prays through the cycle. The participants may meet once a week to discuss their experiences and insights: Which prayers or biblical passages spoke most powerfully to group members? Which readings left them cold or confused? What new insights about God's love or desire for creation—or any promptings to live their faith in a new or different way—came as a result of prayer and reflection?

You may read the prayer book from cover to cover like any other book, though I don't necessarily recommend it. In prayer, as in cooking, there is something to be said for allowing things to simmer or stew. One reader found it helpful to read through a week all at one sitting and then let the images and prayers sift through her consciousness over the next six days. Again, she found her own particular balance between commitment and flexibility.

The Daily Themes and Movements

There is a *thematic* rhythm in the prayer cycle—seven recurring themes, one for each day of the week. Each of these themes is a major topic within the Old and New Testaments, appearing in different forms and contexts from Genesis to Revelation. These themes also recur within the history and practice of Christian prayer and theology, from the beginnings of the faith and into present times. What follows is a brief description of each of the seven themes. (You may want to dog-ear this page to refer to these descriptions as you use the prayer book.)

Monday—Beginnings

The biblical witness assumes and affirms that everything owes its existence, its being, to God. "I believe in God, the Father almighty, *creator* [emphasis added] of heaven and earth," states the Apostles' Creed—and the basis for this affirmation echoes repeatedly from Genesis to Revelation. God is, so to speak, the Great Beginner. From a trinitarian and Christian perspective, the work of creation or creating may be variously ascribed to the Father, Jesus Christ (the Word), or to the Spirit.

Tuesday—God's Providence: Continuing Creation

God's relationship with creation does not *end* with beginnings. The biblical witness affirms that God remains involved in every moment of every day in the life of the world. God's creativity is ongoing, and God's creation continues to unfold. Although the theme of God as Creator (Beginnings) is foundational, more Bible passages refer to this second theme wherein God is actively present, caring and sustaining the life that God has made.

Wednesdays—Wisdom: Creation Teaches

If we look to the created order—even to the smallest forms of life within it—we can learn much about ourselves, about the meaning and purpose of life, and about the God who has made and loves the creation. The splendor of the planets and stars, the intricacy of the human body, or the innate industry of ants all have something to teach us if we listen. The wisdom that creation imparts may inspire us to wonder (e.g., Psalm 19) or leave us humbled and unnerved (e.g., the book of Job).

Thursday—Humankind's Vocation

The scriptures affirm that humanity has a special place and purpose *within* the created order and not apart from it. The biblical witness is varied as to what humanity's role is (e.g., steward, servant, disciple, partner). In my own reading, these roles complement one another rather than contradict.

Friday—Sin and the Destruction of Creation

All is not well within God's created order. The scripture realistically and sometimes ruthlessly depicts human sinfulness: we forget the God who made us; we misuse and abuse others; we abandon our true vocation or calling. From the perspective of the Bible, human sinfulness affects more than the human species; it unravels the fabric of the created order, leading to environmental destruction. Sometimes scripture portrays God as one who uses ecological disaster to call people back to faithfulness (and therefore, God seems to cause or allow bad things to happen). More often, however, the devastation of creation comes as the direct or indirect result of humankind's sinful behavior.

Saturday—God's Recreation

Sin and the destruction of creation do not have the final word, however—in either the Old Testament or the New. God's ultimate (and still unfolding) purpose is toward the blessing of *all* life, human and other-than-human. In the Old Testament, the people of Israel carry this blessing and promise through Abraham and Sarah. God's desire to renew all creation is linked to the renewal or recreation of Israel.

The New Testament views Jesus Christ as the one who brings God's blessing of recreation or resurrection to reality in a unique way as God's own Son, the promised Messiah. "For God so loved the world," John 3:16 says, "that [God] gave his only Son." Jesus embodies the promise made to Abraham and Sarah (that God will bless them and, through them, bless the earth). His life, death, and resurrection impact not only *human* life but the fundamental order of creation.

Sunday—Sabbath: The Praise of Creation

In the first account of creation (Gen. 1:1–2:3), the climax of creation isn't the creation of humankind (day six) but rather the creation of sabbath (day seven)—when God pauses to savor all that God has made. Pausing to rest and delight in God, God's creation, and the gift of life is central to Jewish identity and is reaffirmed throughout scripture.

If we pause to rest and savor, perhaps we will see, hear, or experience how all of life seems held together (apart from our daily efforts) by God—

and how each and every part of creation fulfills God's purpose and blessing. Scripture gives expression to this wholeness by allowing creation itself
to sing, dance, and even applaud God's greatness. To paraphrase Thomas
Merton, a tree, simply by being a tree, praises God. Two people in love, simply by being two people in love, praise God. After this day, the weekly
thematic rhythm begins again.

Each of the times for prayer—Morning, Midday, and Evening—contain set elements or "movements" to assist you. With the exception of a
hymn, Morning and Evening Prayer contain the same movements. Midday
Prayer, intended as a shorter time for prayer, contains only two movements.

Morning and Evening Prayer

Opening

The opening sentences help you make a conscious transition into a time
of prayer, of becoming attuned to God's presence. These sentences may
come from the church's liturgy or hymnody, but most often they come
from either the Old or New Testament. In a way, these words function
like the entryway to a sanctuary: you step off the sidewalk, open the front
door, and enter the place where you have come to meet the Spirit. The
words of the Opening also usher you into the overall theme for the day.

Hymn (Morning Prayer)

Christian worship often includes some form of music or singing, one of
the most powerful expressions of prayer. At the beginning of each Morning
Prayer I offer lyrics from Christian hymns—some old, some new—that
connect with the daily theme. You may sing them aloud, if so moved. If
the hymn is unfamiliar, then you may simply enjoy the prayerful poetry
of the lyrics or make up a tune. ["Sources" lists Catholic and Protestant
hymnals that contain the musical settings for most of these hymns.]

Scripture

We often think of prayer as a time when we speak to God, and this is true.
But prayer is also an act of allowing God to speak to us. For many
Christians, God speaks most powerfully as we read thoughtfully and listen prayerfully to the scriptures of the Old and New Testament. These
scriptures continue both to inform and form us as God's people. They
help us place our own stories within the larger story of God's transform-
ing grace. The central act, therefore, of Morning and Evening Prayer is a
time for engaging the larger story as depicted within scripture.

Here are suggestions for reading the scripture:

1. Read through the passage once, slowly, and perhaps even aloud. Notice any words or images within the scripture for which you have a strong response, either positive or negative.
2. Read through the scripture a second time, letting yourself receive an overall sense of what the passage is talking about.
3. You may decide to read the Bible comment (see page 176) that gives the historical and theological context for the passage. If so, after browsing the commentary, return to the passage for another reading.

Pause for Meditation and Prayer

You are now invited to pause and allow time for meditation upon the scripture. Such meditation is a form of prayer—a way of being open to God's presence. Let the words or images within the scripture enter your imagination gently; pay attention to the feelings and thoughts the scripture engenders. You may find it helpful to write down the words, thoughts, feelings, or images that emerge for you during this meditation.

This "pause" has no set length of time. Make this time of meditation as long as you need in order to feel that you have allowed the text to speak to you personally.

Another Voice

After the time of meditation upon scripture, you are next invited to listen to "another voice" or "voices" from the Christian past or present. These readings may have direct connections with the scripture passage, but more often they simply offer a different perspective on the day's theme.

I quote a variety of sources: some voices are from the Christian past (Augustine, Luther, and Calvin); some are newer voices speaking today (Sallie McFague or Jürgen Moltmann). Sometimes the voice belongs to a community (e.g., the Presbyterian Church U.S.A. or the Iona Community) rather than an individual. Although many of the sources come from Europe and North America, the prayer book also gives voice to those from the Developing World or "South," such as Leonardo Boff (Brazil), Zephania Kameeta (Namibia), or Wangari Maathai (Kenya).

As in the next movement, the purpose served by the variety of voices is to immerse you—slowly, day by day—in the larger witness of the Christian church across the continents and the ages. Many Christians have given much thought and prayer to the interrelationship of God, creation, and humankind; this is an opportunity to hear their "voices."

Prayer

Although all you have been doing up to this point is prayer, at this time I encourage you to speak from your heart *to* God. You may use the given prayer as a way of beginning or ending your personal prayer with God.

Blessing

Just as the opening sentences may help you cross the threshold into prayer, the words of blessing prepare you to leave the sanctuary of Morning or Evening Prayer. I often draw the words of blessing from the words or images just encountered—an image from the scripture, a word from "Another Voice."

Most of the blessings have been composed by me specifically for this prayer book, although sometimes I quote or adapt the blessings of others. Whether the blessings are by me or drawn from another source, I offer them as my prayer, my wish for you in your ongoing life with God.

Midday Prayer

I assume that most readers will pause for Midday Prayer sometime during the course of the workday, perhaps during a break for lunch or coffee. The Midday Prayer, designed for a shorter length of time, offers a single reading followed by a prayer. Feel free to engage in Midday Prayer whenever and however you find it most helpful.

Reflection

Each Midday Prayer begins with a reading or reflection connected to the day's theme. The quotations come from people we do not often hear from in our churches: poets, scientists, naturalists, and cultural prophets. Although many of these authors are Christian, some are not—but they all speak with a voice of love and concern for the earth.

Prayer

Generally, after the reflection, I provide a prayer that connects the reflection more explicitly with the theme of the day and with the Christian faith. The two exceptions are the poem by e. e. cummings (Saturday 1) and the prayer by Thomas Traherne (Tuesday 4); both of these stand alone.

Further Aids for Prayer

Bible Comments

I have supplied brief commentaries on each of the scripture passages. These commentaries are organized according to days of the week and weeks of the month. For example, the commentary on Hosea 2:18-20 is found under "Saturday 2," for this is the day (Saturday) and week (2) in which the passage is quoted in the prayer book.

You can use the prayer book without reading any of the Bible comments. Some people simply allow the scripture passages to speak to them without additional information. However, I often find it helpful to my meditation and prayer to have something more than simply the "bare words" of scripture; I like to know more about the *context* within which these words of scripture occur. This need of mine probably reflects my own background in the Reformed and Presbyterian traditions, wherein a responsible reading of scripture includes a consideration of its historical, literary, and theological context. At any rate, the Bible comments are available if you want or need to know more about a particular passage.

Sources

In the back of the book, I list the source of each quotation or reflection, as well as the translation or version of scripture used. The sources are listed in the order in which they occur within the prayer book.

Drawings

The artist Jane Wageman—a friend and colleague of mine from Mason City, Iowa—has provided original line drawings throughout the body of the prayer book. Walter Burghardt writes that contemplation occurs when we slow down to take "a long, loving look at the real,"[4] and Jane does exactly that whenever she creates her art. Along with the rest of the prayer book, I hope Jane's drawings will encourage you to take "a long, loving look at the real," which is the mystery of God's grace revealed in the creation.

A Note Concerning Language about God and Humankind

One of my chief concerns in *Earth Gospel* is to provide a prayer book that is "theocentric" (God-centered) rather than "anthropocentric" (human-centered). So much damage and suffering have been inflicted on the earth as a result of the presumption (nonbiblical, I quickly add) that the human species, and not God, is the center of everything. Whatever role our species may play in the health and flourishing of creation, the central story always remains God and God's relationship with all of creation, humanity included.

Another fallacy that has caused much damage and suffering is "androcentrism" (male-centered)—another form of anthropocentrism in which the male gender of the human species is regarded as the center of all things. The English language reflects this presumption by the exclusive use of masculine nouns and pronouns to refer to the divine (he, him) and humankind (man, mankind).

Many of the voices from the past that I quote in *Earth Gospel*, including scripture, reflect a male-centered dynamic and language even when inspired by a view of reality that is much broader than any one gender or species. Rather than systematically alter the language for inclusiveness, I have left the language unchanged. On the other hand, I use different translations of scripture throughout *Earth Gospel*, several of which use inclusive language (e.g., *Inclusive-Language Psalms*).

One criteria for my choices of contemporary voices (e.g., Iona Community, Leonardo Boff, Sallie McFague) is their use of inclusive language, as well as their theocentric perspectives. I have also rendered my own prayers, blessings, and translations of scripture in an inclusive style.

While my choices regarding exclusive versus inclusive language may appear inconsistent, there is an underlying logic. I pray that the scripture, meditations, and prayers in *Earth Gospel* will inspire every reader with a view of reality that is much vaster than any one generation, gender, species, language, or planet.

1. For those who wish to learn more about the present environmental crisis I recommend the following excellent resources: William P. Cunningham and Mary Ann Cunningham, *Environmental Science: A Global Concern*, 10th ed. (Burr Ridge, IL: McGraw-Hill, 2007); Jared Diamond, *Collapse: How Societies Choose to Fail or Succeed* (New York: Penguin, 2006); J. R. McNeill, *Something New under the Sun: An Environmental History of the Twentieth-Century World* (New York: W. W. Norton & Company, 2000); James Gustave Speth, *Red Sky at Morning: America and the Crisis of the Global Environment* (New Haven, CT: Yale University Press, 2005).

2. This comes from Calvin's title for his chapter on prayer in his *Institutes of the Christian Religion*, vol. 2, bk. 3, trans. Ford Lewis Battles and ed. John T. McNeill (Philadelphia: Westminster Press, 1960), 20:850.

3. Marjorie J. Thompson, *Soul Feast: An Invitation to the Christian Spiritual Life* (Louisville, KY: Westminster John Knox Press, 1995), 40.

4. Walter J. Burghardt, "Contemplation," in *Church* (Winter 1989): 14.

WEEK ONE

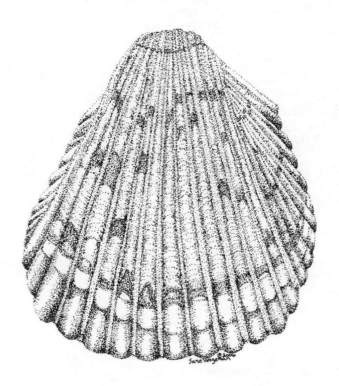

Monday

Beginnings

MORNING

Opening   Joseph Renville (c. 1779–1846)

Many and great, O God, are Thy things,
Maker of earth and sky;
Thy hands set the heavens with stars,
Thy fingers spread the mountains and plains.
Lo, at Thy word the waters were formed;
Deep seas obey Thy voice.

Hymn   "Morning Has Broken"   Eleanor Farjeon, 1931

Morning has broken
Like the first morning,
Blackbird has spoken
Like the first bird.
Praise for the singing!
Praise for the morning!
Praise for them, springing
Fresh from the Word!

Sweet the rain's new fall
Sunlit from heaven,
Like the first dew-fall
On the first grass.
Praise for the sweetness
Of the wet garden,
Sprung in completeness
Where his feet pass.

Mine is the sunlight!
Mine is the morning
Born of the one light
Eden saw play!

Praise with elation,
Praise every morning,
God's recreation
Of the new day!

Scripture   Genesis 1:1-5 (NRSV)

[1] In the beginning when God created the heavens and the earth,
[2] the earth was a formless void and darkness covered the face of the
     deep, while a wind from God swept over the face of the waters.
[3] Then God said, "Let there be light"; and there was light.
[4] And God saw that the light was good; and God separated the
     light from the darkness.
[5] God called the light Day, and the darkness he called Night. And
     there was evening and there was morning, the first day.

A pause for meditation & prayer upon the scripture . . .

Another Voice   Augustine (354–430)

The explanation, then, of the goodness of creation is the goodness
of God.

Prayer   The Anglican Church in Aotearoa, New Zealand and Polynesia

God of unchangeable power,
when you fashioned the world
the morning stars sang together
and the host of heaven shouted for joy;
open our eyes to the wonders of creation
and teach us to use all things for good,
to the honour of your glorious name;
through Jesus Christ our Lord.

Blessing

May you greet
    the goodness of God
in everyone you meet
    in every place you go
    this day.

MIDDAY

Reflection   Wendell Berry

The ecological teaching of the Bible is simply inescapable: God
made the world because He wanted it made. He thinks the world
is good, and He loves it. It is His world; He has never relinquished
title to it. And He has never revoked the conditions, bearing on
His gift to us of the use of it, that oblige us to take excellent care
of it. If God loves the world, then how might any person of faith
be excused for not loving it or justified in destroying it?

Prayer

> Thank you, good God,
> for all the gifts I have already received
> from your creation this day.
> Because the creation is yours
> and you love it,
> help me to love it more dearly.

EVENING

Opening Sentences   Ruth Burgess

> Come among us, Jesus,
> You who hurled the stars into space
> and shaped the spider's weaving.
> Come, Jesus, and meet us here.

Scripture   John 1:1-5 (NRSV)

[1] In the beginning was the Word, and the Word was with God, and
the Word was God. [2] He was in the beginning with God. [3] All
things came into being through him, and without him not one thing
came into being. What has come into being [4] in him was life, and
the life was the light of all people. [5] The light shines in the darkness,
and the darkness did not overcome it.

A pause for meditation & prayer upon the scripture . . .

Another Voice   Kathleen Raine (1908–2003)

Word whose breath is the world-circling atmosphere,
Word that utters the world that turns the wind,
Word that articulates the bird that speeds upon the air,

Word that blazes out the trumpet of the sun,
Whose silence is the violin-music of the stars,
Whose melody is the dawn, and harmony the night,

Word traced in water of lakes, and light on water,
Light on still water, moving water, waterfall
And water colours of cloud, of dew, of spectral rain,

Word inscribed on stone, mountain range upon range of stone,
Word that is fire of the sun and fire within
Order of atoms, crystalline symmetry,

Grammar of five-fold rose and six-fold lily,
Spiral of leaves on a bough, helix of shells,
Rotation of twining plants on axes of darkness and light,

Instinctive wisdom of fish and lion and ram,
Rhythm of generation in flagellate and fern,
Flash of fin, beat of wing, heartbeat, beat of the dance,

Hieroglyph in whose exact precision is defined
Feather and insect-wing, refraction of multiple eyes,
Eyes of the creatures, oh myriadfold vision of the world,

Statement of mystery, how shall we name
A spirit clothed in world, a world made man?

Prayer

Word of life, Jesus Christ,
all creation rests within the grammar of your grace.
May I also rest this night
and so rise ready
to hear your word
tomorrow.

Blessing   *based on* Psalm 121:3-4

> The guardian of Israel
>   never slumbers, never sleeps.
> May God, ever attentive, ever wakeful,
>   keep you this night.

Tuesday

God's Providence: Continuing Creation

MORNING

Opening   Psalm 36:6-8*a* (NAB)

LORD, your love reaches to heaven; *devotion* *faithfulness*
  your fidelity to the clouds.
Your justice is like the highest mountains;
  your judgments, like the mighty deep;
  all living creatures you sustain, LORD.
How precious is your love, O God!

Hymn   "God of the Sparrow"   Jaroslav J. Vajda, 1983

God of the sparrow God of the whale
God of the swirling stars
How does the creature say Awe
How does the creature say Praise

God of the earthquake God of the storm
God of the trumpet blast
How does the creature cry Woe
How does the creature cry Save

God of the rainbow God of the cross
God of the empty grave
How does the creature say Grace
How does the creature say Thanks

God of the hungry God of the sick
God of the prodigal
How does the creature say Care
How does the creature say Life

God of the neighbor God of the foe
God of the pruning hook

How does the creature say Love
How does the creature say Peace

God of the ages God near at hand
God of the loving heart
How do your children say Joy
How do your children say Home

Scripture   Psalm 145:8-9, 13*b*-16 (GRAIL)

[8]   You are kind and full of compassion,
          slow to anger, abounding in love.
[9]   How good you are, Lord, to all,
          compassionate to all your creatures.

[13*b*] You are faithful in all your words
          and loving in all your deeds.
[14]   You support all those who are falling
          and raise up all who are bowed down.
[15]   The eyes of all creatures look to you
          and you give them their food in due time.
[16]   You open wide your hand,
          grant the desires of all who live.

A pause for meditation & prayer upon the scripture . . .

Another Voice   Ruth Page

What, then, would God know and care about, say, a cheetah? Presumably God would know the whole evolutionary history of cheetahs, and the history of this particular cheetah; the cheetah's physical components of particles and molecules; its biological nature as a carnivore and its relation to other big cats; the ecological niche it occupies in the local system; its success or failure in finding food supply, in mating, and in its rearing of cubs (at least if it is a female cheetah). Such knowledge would concern both cheetahs generally and the specific happenings of this particular cheetah's life. God knows how the world looks and smells to a cheetah. Equally the divine presence will see the grace and power of the cheetah at full stretch and prey; will know its frustration at failure and its satisfaction at a successful kill which it can keep from hyenas and other predators.

. . . But God will also know the antelope's experience of the cheetah as predator; the local human beings' view of it, . . . the white hunter's view of it as quarry, with all the hinterland of beliefs and practices which that implies.

. . . From that instance of the cheetah one must extrapolate to all creatures great and small, wild and tame, past, present and future. Yet God's love, like God's presence, is not made thin and general by being offered to all. The divine presence and love is constant and does not admit of degrees, so they are concentrated on each individual at each time, and are as total for non-human beings as for human beings.

Prayer   The Anglican Church in Aotearoa, New Zealand and Polynesia

Let us be aware of the source of being
that is common to us all
and to all living creatures.
>   *Silence*
Let us be filled with the presence of the great compassion
towards ourselves and towards all living beings.
>   *Silence*
Realising that we are all nourished
from the same source of life,
may we so live that others be not deprived
of air, food, water, shelter, or the chance to live.
>   *Silence*

Blessing

The God who creates the cheetah
and provides for its needs,
the Spirit who breathes life into us
and animates our living,
the Word who is recreating all life
each moment, each day,
guide you, feed you,
protect and inspire you
this day.

MIDDAY

Reflection   "The Other"   R. S. Thomas (1913–2000)

There are nights that are so still
that I can hear the small owl calling
far off and a fox barking
miles away. It is then that I lie
in the lean hours awake and listening
to the swell born somewhere in the Atlantic
rising and falling, rising and falling
wave on wave on the long shore
by the village, that is without light
and companionless. And the thought comes
of that other being who is awake, too,
letting our prayers break on him,
not like this for a few hours,
but for days, years, for eternity.

Prayer

You are with me, God,
and with all that lives
not only in the lean hours of the night
nor the rush of new morning,
but now and throughout the day.
Thank you.

EVENING

Opening   Colossians 1:17 (NRSV)

[Christ] himself is before all things,
and in him all things hold together.

Scripture   John 1:14, 16, 18 (NRSV)

[14] And the Word became flesh and lived among us, and we have seen his glory, the glory as of a father's only son, full of grace and truth. . . . [16] From his fullness we have all received, grace upon grace. . . . [18] No one has ever seen God. It is God the only Son, who is close to the Father's heart, who has made him known.

A pause for meditation & prayer upon the scripture . . .

Another Voice   Sallie McFague

Since, for the Christian, God is always incarnate and present, there is no place on earth, no joy or wish that any creature experiences, no need or despair that they suffer, that is not a possible route to God. Wherever reality is seen as hopeful, joyful, and loving, God is there; wherever reality is experienced as despairing, cruel, and hopeless, God must be there also. If God is love, then where love is, God is; where love is not, God must needs be. In nature's health and beauty, I see God; in nature's deterioration and destruction, I see that God is here also. In the first case as a Yes and in the second as No: in the first case as a positive affirmation of God's glory through the flourishing of creation; in the second, as a negative protest against whatever is undermining God's creation.

Prayer   Andrew Linzey

Christ in all things
restore our senses
and give us again
that experience of joy
in all created things.
> Christ in all things:
> in the waves breaking on the shore;
> in the beauty of the sunset;
> in the fragrant blossom of Spring;
> in the music that makes our hearts dance;
> in the kisses of embracing love;
> in the cries of the innocent.

Blessing   J. Philip Newell

Christ stands before me
and peace is in his mind.
Sleep, O sleep
in the calm of all calm
Sleep, O sleep
in the love of all loves
Sleep I this night
in the God of all life.

Wednesday

Wisdom: Creation Teaches

MORNING

Opening   Psalm 145:4-5 (NRSV)

> One generation shall laud your works to another,
>   and shall declare your mighty acts.
> On the glorious splendor of your majesty,
>   and on your wondrous works, I will meditate.

Hymn   "For the Beauty of the Earth"   Folliot Sandford Pierpoint, 1864

> For the beauty of the earth,
> for the glory of the skies,
> for the love which from our birth
> over and around us lies;
> Lord of all, to thee we raise
> this our hymn of grateful praise.
>
> For the beauty of each hour
> of the day and of the night,
> hill and vale, and tree and flower,
> sun and moon, and stars of light;
> Lord of all, to thee we raise
> this our hymn of grateful praise.

Scripture   Psalm 19:2-7 (NAB)

[2]   The heavens declare the glory of God;
        the sky proclaims its builder's craft.
[3]   One day to the next conveys that message;
        one night to the next imparts that knowledge.
[4]   There is no word or sound;
        no voice is heard;
[5]   Yet their report goes forth through all the earth,
        their message, to the ends of the world.

God has pitched there a tent for the sun;
[6]   it comes forth like a bridegroom from his chamber,
          and like an athlete joyfully runs its course.
[7]   From one end of the heavens it comes forth;
          its course runs through to the other;
          nothing escapes its heat.

A pause for meditation & prayer upon the scripture . . .

Another Voice   John Chrysostom (c. 347–407)

[God] hath placed His Creation in the midst,
before the eyes of all men;
in order that they may guess at the Creator from His works. . . .
This it was which the prophet signified when he said,
The heavens declare the glory of God.
How then, tell me, do they declare it?
Voice they have none;
mouth they possess not;
no tongue is theirs!
How then do they declare?
By means of the spectacle itself.
For when thou seest the beauty,
the breadth, the height, the position,
the form, the stability thereof
during so long a period;
hearing as it were a voice,
and being instructed by the spectacle,
thou adorest Him who created
so fair and admirable a body!
The heavens may be silent,
but the sight of them emits a voice,
that is louder than a trumpet's sound.

Prayer   Kathy Galloway, the Iona Community

The sky does it simply, naturally
day by day by day.
The sun does it joyfully,
like someone in love,
like a runner on the starting-line.
The sky, the sun,

they just can't help themselves.
No loud voices, no grand speeches,
but everyone sees, and is happy with them.
Make us like that, Lord,
so that our faith is not in our words but in our lives,
not in what we say but in who we are,
passing on your love like an infectious laugh:
not worried, not threatening, just shining
like the sun, like a starry night,
like a lamp on a stand,
light for life—
your light for our lives.

Blessing

May you see the glory of God in sun and sky;
may you hear the Creator's song in bird and breeze;
and may the grace of Christ's Spirit course through you,
body and soul.

MIDDAY

Reflection   Emily Dickinson (1830–86)

Will there really be a morning?
Is there such a thing as day?
Could I see it from the mountains
If I were as tall as they?

Has it feet like water-lilies?
Has it feathers like a bird?
Is it brought from famous countries
Of which I have never heard?

Oh, some scholar! Oh, some sailor!
Oh, some wise man from the skies!
Please to tell a little pilgrim
Where the place called morning lies!

Prayer

Yours the morning, O God,
yours the afternoon.
As I make my pilgrimage through the day,
reawaken me to your presence,
your wisdom,
your wonders.

EVENING

Opening   Patricia Preece

Lord speak to us
through the beauty of the earth:
from the rising of the sun
till dusk
and the moon and the stars
at night,
your beauty is there
for all to see.

Scripture   Sirach 42:16; 43:1-5 (NRSV)

[42:16] The sun looks down on everything with its light,
and the work of the Lord is full of his glory.

[43:1] The pride of the higher realms is the clear vault of the sky,
as glorious to behold as the sight of the heavens.

[2]   The sun, when it appears, proclaims as it rises
what a marvelous instrument it is,
the work of the Most High.

[3]   At noon it parches the land,
and who can withstand its burning heat?

[4]   A man tending a furnace works in burning heat,
but three times as hot is the sun scorching the mountains;
it breathes out fiery vapors,
and its bright rays blind the eyes.

[5]   Great is the Lord who made it;
at his orders it hurries on its course.

A pause for meditation & prayer upon the scripture . . .

Another Voice   John Calvin (1509–1564)

When we behold the heavens, we cannot but be elevated, by the contemplation of them, to him who is their great Creator; and the beautiful arrangement and wonderful variety which distinguish the courses and station of the heavenly bodies, together with the beauty and splendor which are manifest in them, cannot but furnish us with an evident proof of his providence. Scripture, indeed, makes known to us the time and manner of the creation; but the heavens themselves, although God should say nothing on the subject, proclaim loudly and distinctly enough that they have been fashioned by his hands: and this of itself abundantly suffices to bear testimony to men of his glory. As soon as we acknowledge God to be the supreme Architect, who has erected the beauteous fabric of the universe, our minds must necessarily be ravished with wonder at his infinite goodness, wisdom, and power.

Prayer   Michael Kwatera

> Shine in our darkness, O God,
> as the moon brightens the way
> for mortals and animals.
> As day turns into night,
> turn away from us all evil and harm
> with the power of your Son, Jesus Christ.
> A strong savior is he, for ever and ever. Amen.

Blessing   Norman C. Habel

> May our eyes be blessed that we may see God's beauty in
> the star-swept sky;
> may our ears be blessed that we may hear God calling us
> in the wind;
> may our hearts be blessed that we may feel the love of
> God in the warmth of the sun.
> May God, our Creator, Redeemer, and Sanctifier, bless us
> with each life-renewing breath we take!

Thursday

Humankind's Vocation

MORNING

Opening   Psalm 92:1-2 (NRSV)

It is good to give thanks to the LORD,
    to sing praises to your name, O Most High;
to declare your steadfast love in the morning,
    and your faithfulness at night.

Hymn   "Breathe on Me, Breath of God"   Edwin Hatch, 1886

Breathe on me, Breath of God,
Fill me with life anew,
That I may love what Thou dost love,
And do what Thou wouldst do.

Breathe on me, Breath of God,
Until my heart is pure,
Until with Thee I will one will,
To do and to endure.

Breathe on me, Breath of God,
Till I am wholly Thine,
Until this earthly part of me
Glows with Thy fire divine.

Scripture   Genesis 1:24-31 (NRSV)

[24] And God said, "Let the earth bring forth living creatures of every kind: cattle and creeping things and wild animals of the earth of every kind." And it was so. [25] God made the wild animals of the earth of every kind, and the cattle of every kind, and everything that creeps upon the ground of every kind. And God saw that it was good.
[26] Then God said, "Let us make humankind in our image, according to our likeness; and let them have dominion over the fish of the sea,

and over the birds of the air, and over the cattle, and over all the wild animals of the earth, and over every creeping thing that creeps upon the earth."

[27] So God created humankind in his image,
in the image of God he created them;
male and female he created them.

[28] God blessed them, and God said to them, "Be fruitful and multiply, and fill the earth and subdue it; and have dominion over the fish of the sea and over the birds of the air and over every living thing that moves upon the earth." [29] God said, "See, I have given you every plant yielding seed that is upon the face of all the earth, and every tree with seed in its fruit; you shall have them for food. [30] And to every beast of the earth, and to every bird of the air, and to everything that creeps on the earth, everything that has the breath of life, I have given every green plant for food." And it was so. [31] God saw everything that he had made, and indeed, it was very good. And there was evening and there was morning, the sixth day.

A pause for meditation & prayer upon the scripture . . .

Other Voices   Presbyterian Church (U.S.A.)
from *Restoring Creation for Ecology and Justice*

The fundamental claim that the earth is God's creation means that those who acknowledge the claim are bound to relate to the natural world with respect and care. "God saw everything that [God] had made, and behold, it was very good" (Gen. 1:31). The creation has value simply because it is God's creation. And people who understand themselves as God's people cannot treat carelessly or destructively God's world, in which God delights.

Sallie McFague

The message of Genesis
is not domination but appreciation.
We who the text says are made in God's image
ought to reflect God's attitude toward nature: appreciation.

Prayer   The Evangelical Reformed Churches in German-speaking
Switzerland (1972)

Lord, you love life; we owe our existence to you.
Give us reverence for life and love for every
creature. Sharpen our senses so that we shall
recognize the beauty and also the longing of
your creation, and, as befits your children, treat
our fellow creatures of the animal and plant kingdoms
with love as our brothers and sisters, in readiness for
your great day, when you will make all things new.

Blessing   Ray Simpson, Community of Aidan and Hilda

God bless the earth that is beneath us
The sky that is above us
The day that lies before us
Your image deep within us.

MIDDAY

Reflection   Loren Eiseley (1907–1977)

I was away from the shellers now and strode more rapidly over the wet
sand that effaced my footprints. Around the next point there might be
a refuge from the wind. The sun behind me was pressing upward at the
horizon's rim—an ominous red glare amidst the tumbling blackness of
the clouds. Ahead of me, over the projecting point, a gigantic rainbow of
incredible perfection had sprung shimmering into existence. Somewhere
toward its foot I discerned a human figure standing, as it seemed to me,
within the rainbow, though unconscious of his position. He was gazing
fixedly at something in the sand.

Eventually he stooped and flung the object beyond the breaking surf.
I labored toward him over a half-mile of uncertain footing. By the time
I reached him the rainbow had receded ahead of us, but something of its
color still ran hastily in many changing lights across his features. He was
starting to kneel again.

In a pool of sand and silt a starfish had thrust its arms up stiffly and
was holding its body away from the stifling mud.

"It's still alive," I ventured.

"Yeah," he said, and with a quick yet gentle movement he picked up the star and spun it over my head and far out into the sea. It sank in a burst of spume, and the waters roared once more.

"It may live," he said, "if the offshore pull is strong enough." He spoke gently, and across his bronzed worn face the light still came and went in subtly altering colors.

"There are not many come this far," I said, groping in a sudden embarrassment for words. "Do you collect?"

"Only like this," he said softly, gesturing amidst the wreckage of the shore.

"And only for the living." He stooped again, oblivious of my curiosity, and skipped another star neatly across the water.

"The stars," he said, "throw well. One can help them."

He looked full at me with a faint question kindling in his eyes, which seemed to take on the far depths of the sea.

Prayer

Star-flinging Spirit,
you stop, stoop, kneel, and embrace
everyone and everything in need of your love and care.
May I join you today in caring for your creation,
embracing my role within the family of life.

EVENING

Opening   Charles Wesley, 1740

> Expand thy wings, celestial Dove,
> brood o'er our nature's night;
> on our disordered spirits move,
> and let there now be light.

Scripture   Genesis 2:4-8, 15   Trans. by Mary Phil Korsak

[4] These are the breedings of the skies and the earth
     at their creation
     On the day YHWH Elohim made earth and skies

[5] no shrub of the field was yet in the earth
     no plant of the field had yet sprouted
     for YHWH Elohim had not made it rain on the earth
     and there was no groundling to serve the ground
[6] But a surge went up from the earth
     and gave drink to all the face of the ground
[7] YHWH Elohim formed the groundling, soil of the ground He
     blew into its nostrils the blast of life
     and the groundling became a living soul

[8] YHWH Elohim planted a garden in Eden in the east
     There he set the groundling he had formed

[15] YHWH Elohim took the groundling
     and set it to rest in the garden of Eden
     to serve it and keep it.

A pause for meditation & prayer upon the scripture . . .

Another Voice   World Council of Churches

> The divine presence of the Spirit in creation
> binds us as human beings
> together with all created life.
> We are accountable before God
> in and to the community of life,
> an accountability which has been imaged

in various ways:
as servants,
stewards and trustees,
as tillers and keepers,
as priests of creation,
as nurturers,
as co-creators.
This requires attitudes of compassion and humility,
respect and reverence.

Prayer   The Royal Society for the Prevention of Cruelty to Animals

Heavenly Father
your Holy Spirit
gives breath to all living things;
renew us by this same Spirit
that we may learn to respect
what you have given
and care for what you have made
through Jesus Christ
your Son, our Lord.

Blessing

In your breathing,
in your sleeping,
in your dreaming,
may the breath of God
fill you, body and soul.

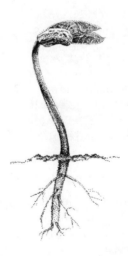

Friday

Sin and the Destruction of Creation

MORNING

Opening   Lutheran World Federation   *Henri Nouwen book*

Christ, our wounded healer

[suffering the pains of creation,

lead us back to the tree of life, → *Eden*

to the source of healing for the Earth.

Hymn   *from* "Come, Lord, and Tarry Not"   Horatius Bonar (1808–1889)

Come, Lord, and tarry not;
Bring the long-looked-for day;
O why these years of waiting here,
These ages of delay?

Come, for creation groans,
Impatient of Thy stay,
Worn out with these long years of ill,
These ages of delay.

Come and make all things new;
Build up this ruined earth;
Restore our faded Paradise,
(Creation's second birth.) → *What will this be like? — a new Eden.*

Scripture   Jeremiah 12:10-13 (NRSV)

[10] Many shepherds have destroyed my vineyard,
      they have trampled down my portion,
   they have made my pleasant portion
      a desolate wilderness.
[11] They have made it a desolation;
      desolate, it mourns to me.
   The whole land is made desolate,   *when this*
      but no one lays it to heart.   *was written*
      Jeremiah didn't
      know the half of desolation

[12] Upon all the bare heights in the desert
    spoilers have come;
for the sword of the LORD devours
    from one end of the land to the other;
    no one shall be safe.
[13] They have sown wheat and have reaped thorns, *How often*
    they have tired themselves out but profit nothing. *have we*
They shall be ashamed of their harvests *felt like*
    because of the fierce anger of the LORD. *this*

A pause for meditation & prayer upon the scripture . . .

Another Voice   Ecumenical Patriarch Bartholomew I

The root cause of all our difficulties lies in human selfishness and human sin. *What is asked of us is not greater technological skill but deeper repentance, or metanoia,* which in the literal sense of the Greek word signifies "change of mind." The root cause of our environmental sin lies in our self-centeredness and in the mistaken order of values that we inherit and accept without any critical evaluation. We need a new way of thinking about our own selves, about our relationship with the world and with God. Without this revolutionary "change of mind," all our conservation projects, however well intentioned, will remain ultimately ineffective. For we shall be dealing only with the symptoms, not with their cause. Lectures and international conferences may help to awaken our conscience, but what is truly required is a baptism of tears.

We, God's glorious creation, have destroyed His creation. Indian with tear

Prayer   U.N. Environmental Sabbath

Great Spirit, give us hearts to understand; *How do*
never to take from creation's beauty more than we give; *we survive*
never to destroy wantonly for the furtherance of greed; *without harming*
never to deny to give our hands *the earth*
for the building of Earth's beauty; *further?*
never to take from her what we cannot use.
Give us hearts to understand
    that to destroy Earth's music is to create confusion;
    that to wreck her appearance is to blind us to beauty;
    that to callously pollute her fragrance
    is to make a house of stench;
    that as we care for her she will care for us. Amen.

Blessing   Peter W. Millar; *adapted*

> May the good Lord show you
> how to be frugal, till all are fed;
> how to weep, till all can laugh;
> how to be meek, till all can stand in pride;
> how to mourn, till all are comforted;
> how to be restless, till all live in peace;
> how to claim less, till all find justice.
> Then you will be blessed indeed
> and the earth itself will be blessed
> through you.

MIDDAY

Reflection   "Tragic Error"   Denise Levertov (1923–97)

> *The earth is the Lord's,* we gabbled,
> *and the fullness thereof*—
> while we looted and pillaged, claiming indemnity:
> *the fullness thereof*
> *given over to us, to our use*—
> while we preened ourselves, sure of our power,
> wilful or ignorant, through the centuries.
>
> Miswritten, misread, that charge:
> *subdue* was the false, the misplaced word in the story.
> Surely we were to have been
> earth's mind, mirror, reflective source.
> Surely our task
> was to have been
> to love the earth,
> to *dress and keep it* like Eden's garden.
>
> *That* would have been our *dominion*:
> to be those cells of earth's body that could
> perceive and imagine, could bring the planet
> into the haven it is to be known,
> (as the eye blesses the hand, perceiving
> its form and the work it can do).

Prayer

Set me free, O God,
from my empire-prison
of human self-importance.
Help me to serve you and your creation
with energy, intelligence, imagination, and love.

EVENING

Opening   Psalm 51:10-11 (NRSV)

Create in me a clean heart, O God,
    and put a new and right spirit within me.
Do not cast me away from your presence,
    and do not take your holy spirit from me.

Scripture   Psalm 107:33-43 (ILP)

[33] God turns rivers into a desert,
        springs of water into thirsty ground,
[34] a fruitful land into a salty waste,
        because of the wickedness of its inhabitants. . . .

[35] God turns a desert into pools of water,
        a parched land into springs of water.
[36] And there God lets the hungry dwell,
        and they establish a city to live in;
[37] they sow fields, and plant vineyards,
        and get a fruitful yield. . . .
[38] They multiply greatly by the blessing of God,
        who does not let their cattle decrease.
[39] When they are diminished and brought low
        through oppression, trouble, and sorrow,
[40] God pours contempt upon princes
        and makes them wander in tractless wastes;
[41] but God raises up those who are needy out of
        affliction, and makes their families like flocks. . . .

[42] The upright see it and are glad;
      and all wickedness stops its mouth.
[43] Whoever is wise should give heed to these things;
      let people consider the steadfast love of God.

A pause for meditation & prayer upon the scripture . . .

Another Voice   Leonardo Boff

Astronauts who travelled into space and recorded their impressions of the earth described it as a ship on a voyage. In fact, in this ship which is the earth a fifth of the population are travelling in first class and in luxury class; they enjoy all the benefits. They consume 80 percent of the resources available for the voyage. The remaining 80 percent of the passengers are travelling steerage. They suffer cold, hunger, and all kinds of privations. Many ask why they are travelling steerage. Need forces others to rebel. It is not difficult to see what is at stake. Either everyone can be saved in a system of communal solidarity and participation on the ship—and ~~in that case fundamental changes are necessary~~—or, as a result ~~of outrage~~ and revolt, the ship will explode and throw everyone into the sea. This awareness is growing throughout the world.

Prayer   "Waste"   Stephen Orchard

Not only in ancient ruined cities
but in and around the modern city
are the waste-heaps and garbage of our lives,
picked over by the foxes and the crows
and the human scavengers who make a living there.

Forgive us, Lord, for mentioning
     our rubbish in our prayers.
     We would rather enjoy the fruits of creation
      and forget about the consequences.
Forgive us our polluted water,
     our toxic soil and sulphurous air.
Forgive us all the dumped surpluses,
     the slag heaps and the piles of scrap.
We thank you for the signs of your forgiveness;
for the plants and trees which colonise
even the most unsightly ground;
for the animals and birds who learn to live

in secret places in our urban sprawl
and turn our rubbish to good account.

We thank you for those who deal with our rubbish,
who keep our streets and houses healthy;
who guard us against poisons and radiation,
or who turn our waste into new riches.

We pray for those for whom the rubbish tip
is the only source of food and wealth,
picking through others' leavings in the search
to keep their family alive.

*Most generous giver, from whose creation there is enough for all and to
spare, make us wise stewards of the earth's treasure and generous in
our turn to one another.*

Blessing

Within the economy of God's grace,
nothing is ever wasted
and no one thrown away.
May you entrust yourself
and God's creation
to the power and peace
of Christ's recycling love.

Saturday

God's Recreation

MORNING

Opening   Isaiah 12:3-4 (NRSV)

With joy you will draw water from the wells of salvation. And
you will say in that day:
>   Give thanks to the LORD,
>   call on his name;
>   make known his deeds among the nations;
>   proclaim that his name is exalted.

Hymn   *from* "When Morning Gilds the Skies"
German Hymn (c. 1800) Trans. Edward Caswall, 1853, 1858; alt.

>   When morning gilds the skies,
>   My heart awaking cries:
>   May Jesus Christ be praised!
>   Alike at work and prayer
>   To Jesus I repair:
>   May Jesus Christ be praised!

>   Let earth's wide circle round
>   In joyful notes resound:
>   May Jesus Christ be praised!
>   Let air and sea and sky
>   From depth to height reply:
>   May Jesus Christ be praised!

Scripture   Psalm 145 (BARNETT)

[1]   My sovereign God, I must exalt you;
        I must bless your Name for ever and ever.
[2]   Every day I will bless you
        and everlastingly praise your Name.

[3]   Great are you, Holy One,
          most worthy of praise,
          grand beyond all knowing.

[4]   Generation on generation shall praise your works
          and proclaim your mighty power.
[5]   They will declare your glorious majesty.
          I will meditate on your marvelous works.
[6]   They will speak of the power of your awesome acts.
          I will proclaim your greatness.
[7]   They will pour out memories of your great goodness
          and loudly praise your true justice.

[8]   You are gracious and merciful,
          slow to anger, and filled with faithful love.
[9]   You, O Holy One, are good to everyone;
          compassion abounds in your every act.
[10] All your works praise you;
          your loving, faithful people bless you.
[11] They talk of the glory of your majesty
          and speak of the honor of your reign,
[12]   to teach all peoples your mighty power
          and the majesty of your reign.
[13] Your reign is for all eternity,
          your dominion for all generations.
      You are truthful in all your words;
          your works show faithful love.

[14] You lift up all who fall,
          and restore those who are prostrate.
[15] All eyes look to you with hope
          and you give them food in due season.
[16] You open your hand
          and satisfy the desire of every living thing.

[17] Holy One, you are faithful and just in all your ways,
          true and loving in all your works.
[18] You are close to all who call to you,
          to all who call sincerely.

[19] You meet the needs of all who revere you.
          You hear their cries for help and rescue them.
[20] You protect all who love you,
          but destroy the wicked.

Let my mouth praise you, O Holy One,
   and all flesh bless God's Holy Name.
Forever and forever!

A pause for meditation & prayer upon the scripture . . .

Another Voice   Presbyterian Church (U.S.A.)
from *Restoring Creation for Ecology and Justice*

In this psalm of praise [Psalm 145] the themes of creation, care,
and deliverance are thoroughly intertwined. Because the Lord's
compassion extends to all that God has made, we should not think
the deliverance of all who are bowed down refers only to human
beings. Because God satisfies the desire of every living thing, those
whom God saves may be other forms of life, not only people.

Prayer

Praise to you, my God and Creator!
Your creativity is matched by your compassion!
Today is a new day in the life of creation.
Let me see and hear,
taste, touch, and smell
the thrill of your grace
the pulse of the Spirit
in and through all creation.

Blessing   Janet Morley

May the God who dances in creation,
who embraces us with human love,
who shakes our lives like thunder,
bless us and drive us out with power
to fill the world with her justice,
        Amen.

MIDDAY

Reflection and Prayer e. e. cummings (1894–1962)

i thank You God for most this amazing
day: for the leaping greenly spirits of trees
and a blue true dream of sky; and for everything
which is natural which is infinite which is yes
(i who have died am alive again today,
and this is the sun's birthday; this is the birth
day of life and of love and wings; and of the gay
great happening illimitably earth)

how should tasting touching hearing seeing
breathing any—lifted from the no
of all nothing—human merely being
doubt unimaginable You?

(now the ears of my ears awake and
now the eyes of my eyes are opened)

EVENING

Opening *from* "Psalm" Julia Esquivel

I have been summoned by Love!
Real love that believes and hopes and discovers
because it is stronger than death.

It comes to us from beyond the zenith
and submerges itself into the depth of the nadir.

Love that extends my arms into the infinite
and invites me to embrace the cosmos with its tenderness.

Scripture John 3:16-17 (NRSV)

[16] "For God so loved the world that he gave his only Son, so that
everyone who believes in him may not perish but may have eternal life.

[17] "Indeed, God did not send the Son into the world to condemn the world, but in order that the world might be saved through him."

A pause for meditation & prayer upon the scripture . . .

Other Voices   Catherine of Siena (1347–80)

The reason why God's servants love [God's] creatures so deeply is that they realize how deeply Christ loves them. And it is the very character of love to love what is loved by those we love.

Sallie McFague

There is only one world,
a world that God loves.
Since God loves it,
we not only *can* but *should*.
In fact, loving the world (not God alone),
or rather, loving God *through* loving the world,
is the Christian way.

[handwritten margin note:] So, we profess our love for God - we live Him by loving others - loving you. We say we love back (others), we intercede in prayer for one another, but does it end there? What do we do for one another. Do we share out + support one another by listening to hopes, dreams & fears.

Prayer   Ray Simpson, Community of Aidan and Hilda

Jesus—
Truly God, truly human
Truly infinite, truly frail
Your greatness holds the universe
Your lovely countenance attracts our hearts
Your goodness beckons all that is good in us
Your wisdom searches us
Your truth sheds light on our darkness
Your generosity enriches our poverty
Your friendship consoles the unwanted
Your strength turns away all evils
Your justice deters wrong-doing
Your power conquers hell
Your love-enflamed heart kindles our cold hearts
Your miraculous hand fills us with all blessings
Your sweet and holy name rejoices all who love you
Your mercy brings forgiveness.
Have mercy on us

[handwritten margin note:] What have I done for you lately?

Give us eternal life
For your glory fills eternity;
Your glory fills the universe.

Blessing

May the risen Christ
who fills all creation
with his glory and grace,
fill you tonight with his peace.

Sunday

Sabbath: The Praise of Creation

MORNING

Opening   Isaiah 66:23 (NRSV)

> From new moon to new moon,
>   and from sabbath to sabbath,
> all flesh shall come to worship before me,
>   says the LORD.

Hymn   "For the Earth Forever Turning"   Kim Oler

> For the earth forever turning;
> For the skies, for every sea;
> To the Lord we sing returning
> Home to our blue green hills of earth.
>
> For the mountains, hills and pastures
> In their silent majesty;
> For all life, for all of Nature
> Sing we our joyful praise to Thee.
>
> For the sun, for rain and thunder;
> For the land that makes us free;
> For the stars, for all the heavens,
> Sing we our joyful praise to Thee.
>
> For the earth forever turning;
> For the skies, for every sea;
> To our Lord we sing returning
> Home to our blue green hills of earth.

Scripture   Genesis 2:1-3 (NRSV)

[1] Thus the heavens and the earth were finished, and all their multitude. [2] And on the seventh day God finished the work that he had done, and he rested on the seventh day from all the work that he had done. [3] So God blessed the seventh day and hallowed it, because on it God rested from all the work that he had done in creation.

A pause for meditation & prayer upon the scripture . . .

Another Voice   Jürgen Moltmann

According to the biblical Jewish and Christian traditions, God created the world for his glory, out of love; and the crown of creation is not the human being; it is the sabbath. It is true that, as the image of God, the human being has his special position in creation. But he stands together with all other earthly and heavenly beings in the same hymn of praise of God's glory, and in the enjoyment of God's sabbath pleasure over creation, as he saw that it was good. Even without human beings, the heavens declare the glory of God.

Prayer   The Brothers of Weston Priory

Creator Spirit,
mighty wind of God,
You brood over our lives,
and speak new life into our chaos.
You set Your Sabbath apart for Your service.

Your Sabbath
celebrates the flowering of creation,
the wedding of our hopes
to Your divine yearning.
In the light of your holy Sabbath,
each day is holy;
in the overflowing of Sabbath joy,
each moment is sacred.

As we read in the story of creation:
"Now the whole universe
—sky, earth, and all their array
—was completed.
With the seventh day,
God enjoyed rest from the labor of creation.
Then God blessed the seventh day,
and called it holy."

Overshadow us now
with your beauty and your joy,
that our world may know
a Sabbath of wholeness and peace,
today and forever.

Blessing

May God's own goodness
and the goodness of God's creation
fill you with so much joy
that you cannot keep from singing.

MIDDAY

Reflection   "Saint Francis and the Sow"   Galway Kinnell

The bud
stands for all things,
even for those things that don't flower,
for everything flowers, from within, of self-blessing;
though sometimes it is necessary
to reteach a thing its loveliness,
to put a hand on its brow
of the flower
and retell it in words and in touch
it is lovely
until it flowers again from within, of self-blessing;
as Saint Francis
put his hand on the creased forehead

of the sow, and told her in words and in touch
blessings of earth on the sow, and the sow
began remembering all down her thick length,
from the earthen snout all the way
through the fodder and slops to the spiritual curl of the tail,
from the hard spininess spiked out from the spine
down through the great broken heart
to the sheer blue milken dreaminess spurting and shuddering
from the fourteen teats into the fourteen mouths sucking and
　　blowing beneath them:
the long, perfect loveliness of sow.

Prayer

Each day, every moment,
you place your hand of blessing
upon the brow of creation.
In your touch, in your words,
everything flowers,
everything remembers
the deep, perfect loveliness within.
The deep, perfect loveliness of you.

EVENING

Opening　　Michael Kwatera

With all that has wings—
with birds and bugs,
with bats and bees and butterflies—
we lift our praise above, Lord God.

Scripture　　Psalm 131 (NAB)

[1]　LORD, my heart is not proud;
　　　　nor are my eyes haughty.
　　　I do not busy myself with great matters,
　　　　with things too sublime for me.

[2]   Rather, I have stilled my soul,
        hushed it like a weaned child.
      Like a weaned child on its mother's lap,
        so is my soul within me.
[3]   Israel, hope in the LORD,
        now and forever.

A pause for meditation & prayer upon the scripture . . .

Another Voice   Mother Teresa of Calcutta (1910–97)

We need to find God and God cannot be found in noise and
restlessness. God is the friend of silence. See how nature—trees and
flowers and grass—grow in silence. See the stars, the moon and the
sun, how they move in silence. The more we receive in silent prayer,
the more we can give in our active life.

Prayer   The Anglican Church in Aotearoa, New Zealand and Polynesia

    Loving creator of all,
    watch over us this night
    and keep us in the light of your presence.
    May our praise continually blend
    with the song of all creation,
    until we come to those eternal joys
    which you promise in your love;
    through Jesus Christ our Saviour.
    Amen.

Blessing   *based on* 2 Thessalonians 3:16

    May the Lord, who is our peace,
    give us peace at all times and in every way.

WEEK TWO

Monday

Beginnings

MORNING

Opening   Isaiah 44:24 (NRSV)

> Thus says the LORD your Redeemer,
>> who formed you in the womb:
> I am the LORD, who made all things,
>> who alone stretched out the heavens,
>> who by myself spread out the earth.

Hymn   "God Created Heaven and Earth"   Taiwanese Hymn
Trans. Boris and Clare Anderson, 1981

> God created heaven and earth,
> All things perfect brought to birth;
> God's great power made dark and light,
> Earth revolving day and night.

> Let us praise God's mercy great,
> All our needs that love await;
> God, who fashions all that lives,
> To each one a blessing gives.

Scripture   Isaiah 40:12-15 (NRSV)

[12]   Who has measured the waters in the hollow of his hand
        and marked off the heavens with a span,
    enclosed the dust of the earth in a measure,
        and weighed the mountains in scales
        and the hills in a balance?
[13]   Who has directed the spirit of the LORD,
        or as his counselor has instructed him?

[14] Whom did he consult for his enlightenment,
          and who taught him the path of justice?
       Who taught him knowledge,
          and showed him the way of understanding?
[15] Even the nations are like a drop from a bucket,
          and are accounted as dust on the scales;
       see, he takes up the isles like fine dust.

A pause for meditation & prayer upon the scripture . . .

Another Voice   Martin Luther (1483–1546)

God is substantially present everywhere,
in and through all creatures, in all their parts and places,
so that the world is full of God and He fills all,
but without His being encompassed and surrounded by it.
He is at the same time outside and above all creatures.
These are all exceedingly incomprehensible matters;
yet they are articles of our faith and are attested clearly and
       mightily in Holy Writ. . . .
For how can reason tolerate it that the Divine Majesty is so small
that it can be substantially present in a grain [of wheat],
on a grain, over a grain, through a grain,
within and without, and that, although it is a single Majesty,
it nevertheless is entirely in each grain separately,
no matter how immeasurably numerous these grains may be? . . .
His own divine essence can be in all creatures collectively
and in each one individually more profoundly, more intimately,
more present than the creature is in itself.

Prayer   Uniting Church in Australia

Gracious God,
We praise you for the marvels of your creation,
       for plants growing in earth and water,
       the life inhabiting lakes and seas,
       for all that creeps through the soils and land,
       for all creatures in the wetlands and waterways,
       for life flying above earth and sea
       for the diversity and beauty of your creation
we stand in awe and wonder.

Blessing

May the One who can scoop the ocean with one hand—
the One who is profoundly present to each grain of sand—
hold you firmly
and carry you gently
this day.

MIDDAY

Reflection   Annie Dillard

The world is full of creatures that for some reason seem stranger to us than others . . . hagfish, platypuses, lizardlike pangolins four feet long with bright green, lapped scales like umbrella-tree leaves on a bush hut roof, butterflies emerging from anthills, spiderlings wafting through the air clutching tiny silken balloons, horseshoe crabs . . . the creator creates. Does he stoop, does he speak, does he save, succor, prevail? Maybe. But he creates; he creates everything and anything.

. . . The creator goes off on one wild, specific tangent after another, or millions simultaneously, with an exuberance that would seem to be unwarranted, and with an abandoned energy sprung from an unfathomable font. What is going on here? The point of the dragonfly's terrible lip, the giant water bug, birdsong, or the beautiful dazzle and flash of sunlighted minnows, is not that it all fits together like clockwork—for it doesn't, particularly, not even inside the goldfish bowl—but that it all flows so freely wild, like the creek, that it all surges in such a free, fringed tangle. Freedom is the world's water and weather, the world's nourishment freely given, its soil and sap: and the creator loves pizzazz.

Prayer

Set me free, O God,
to go off with you today
on one wild, specific tangent after another,
immersed and amazed
in the wonder
and even terror
of your immense
creative beauty.

EVENING

Opening   Geoff Lowson, United Society for the Proclamation
of the Gospel

O Lord our God,
Whose righteousness is like the strong mountains
and whose justice is as the great deep:
Let us know your presence now.

O Lord our God,
whose power girds the mountains,
whose hands cradle the hills and yet whose mercy is boundless:
Let us know your presence now.

O Lord our God,
whose glory is greater than our understanding
and whose love cannot be measured:
Let us know your presence now.

Scripture   Romans 11:33-36 (NRSV)

[33] O the depth of the riches and wisdom and knowledge of God!
How unsearchable are his judgments and how inscrutable his ways!
[34] "For who has known the mind of the Lord?
      Or who has been his counselor?"
[35] "Or who has given a gift to him,
      to receive a gift in return?"
[36] For from him and through him and to him are all things. To him
be the glory forever. Amen.

A pause for meditation & prayer upon the scripture . . .

Another Voice   Barbara Wood

The more scientists discover about the world in which we live and the
organization of different forms of life, the more it becomes clear that the
generosity and abundance with which God's creation is endowed is a far
cry from the meanness of chance, utility and accident. It is now realized
that the conditions in which our universe came into being were so extra-
ordinary that, but for split-second timing, it would not have been possible for it to have developed the way it has. The intricacy of the organization

of nature speaks of a profound design and mind behind it. There is care at every stage and every step of the creative process. Each new creation follows on from the next, is dependent on the rest of creation. . . .

Evolution as the instrument of God's purpose, rather than as accident, takes on quite a different meaning. Instead of leading us to accept aggression and violence as necessary for survival, it takes us in the opposite direction: we become united to all the strivings and strainings of creation.

Everything we are, we have received through the struggles of thousands of species of living creatures: our eyes with which we observe God's creation, our ears with which we hear God's praises sung by all creation, our bodies with which we move and work and experience pleasures and pain.

Prayer   Gregory Nazianzen (c. 330–389)

You alone are unutterable
from the time you created all things that can be spoken of.
You alone are unknowable
from the time you created all things that can be known.
All things cry out about you
    those which speak, and those which cannot speak,
all things honour you
    those which think, and those which cannot think.
For there is one longing, one groaning, that all things have for you.
All things pray to you . . .
and offer you a silent hymn.
In you, the One, all things abide
and all things endlessly run to you
who are the end of all.

Blessing

Today, tonight
God's purpose in every stage,
every step, every life.
Today, tonight
God's praise on every tongue,
every ear, every prayer,
and in every dream.

Tuesday

God's Providence: Continuing Creation

MORNING

Opening   *based on* Hosea 6:3

> With the rising of the sun,
> let us seek to know God,
> whose coming is as sure as dawn,
> whose grace is like rain,
> renewing the face of the earth.

Hymn   "I Sing the Mighty Power of God"   Isaac Watts, 1715; alt.

> I sing the goodness of the Lord
> That filled the earth with food;
> God formed the creatures with a word
> And then pronounced them good.
> Lord, how Thy wonders are displayed,
> Where're I turn my eyes;
> If I survey the ground I tread,
> Or gaze upon the skies!
>
> There's not a plant or flower below
> But makes Thy glories known;
> And clouds arise, and tempests blow,
> By order from Thy throne;
> While all that borrows life from Thee
> Is ever in Thy care,
> And everywhere that we can be,
> Thou, God, art present there.

Scripture   Psalm 104:1-2*a*, 10-24 (NRSV)

[1]   Bless the LORD, O my soul.
        O LORD my God, you are very great.
    You are clothed with honor and majesty,
[2]   wrapped in light as with a garment.

[10]   You make springs gush forth in the valleys;
        they flow between the hills,
[11]   giving drink to every wild animal;
        the wild asses quench their thirst.
[12]   By the streams the birds of the air have their habitation;
        they sing among the branches.
[13]   From your lofty abode you water the mountains;
        the earth is satisfied with the fruit of your work.
[14]   You cause the grass to grow for the cattle,
        and plants for people to use,
    to bring forth food from the earth,
[15]   and wine to gladden the human heart,
    oil to make the face shine,
        and bread to strengthen the human heart.
[16]   The trees of the LORD are watered abundantly,
        the cedars of Lebanon that he planted.
[17]   In them the birds build their nests;
        the stork has its home in the fir trees.
[18]   The high mountains are for the wild goats;
        the rocks are a refuge for the coneys.
[19]   You have made the moon to mark the seasons;
        the sun knows its time for setting.
[20]   You make darkness, and it is night,
        when all the animals of the forest come creeping out.
[21]   The young lions roar for their prey,
        seeking their food from God.
[22]   When the sun rises, they withdraw
        and lie down in their dens.
[23]   People go out to their work
        and to their labor until the evening.
[24]   O LORD, how manifold are your works!
        In wisdom you have made them all;
        the earth is full of your creatures.

A pause for meditation & prayer upon the scripture . . .

Other Voices   Catholic Bishops of the Pacific Northwest

Creation is a "book of nature" in whose living pages people can see signs of the Spirit of God present in the universe, yet separate from it. . . .

Each portion of creation can be sign and revelation for the person of faith, a moment of grace revealing God's presence to us.

Samuel Rayan

The earth is the Lord's, for it is the Lord's self-manifestation.
It is something God is saying and doing,
an ongoing revelation, an unfolding word of God
in which something of God's thought and heart are disclosed. . . .
The earth, then, is a revealed word of God,
always alive and fresh,
never frozen into human words which age and die. . . .
The earth and everything in it are loving and saving words
addressed to us and addressing each other.
God says it all with rainbows and flowers,
with rice and wheat, and the glory of sunsets,
the charm of children, the beauty of brides,
the innovativeness of youth and the prayers of trees,
the mystery of silent things and the joy of friendship.

Prayer

Yours the seed, yours the growth;
yours the water, yours the thirst;
yours the wild, yours the tame.
You are within me, O God,
and within all creation—
and you are beyond.
Shape and fill me this day
and all creation
with your grace.

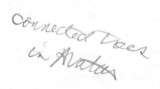

Blessing   *based on* Psalm 1:3

May you stand like a tree
planted by a stream,
bearing fruit in season,
your leaves never fading,
your yield always plenty.

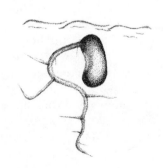

MIDDAY

Reflection   Henry David Thoreau (1817–62)

My profession is to be always on the alert to find God in nature, to know [God's] lurking places, to attend all the oratorios, the operas, in nature.

Prayer

> Keep me awake, alert, and attentive
> to the unfolding music of your grace
> all around me
> and within.

EVENING

Opening   Isaiah 61:11 (NAB)

> As the earth brings forth its plants,
>   and a garden makes its growth spring up,
> So will the Lord GOD make justice and praise
>   spring up before all the nations.

Scripture   Genesis 8:20-22 (NRSV)

[20] Then Noah built an altar to the LORD, and took of every clean animal and of every clean bird, and offered burnt offerings on the altar. [21] And when the LORD smelled the pleasing odor, the LORD said in his heart, "I will never again curse the ground because of humankind, for the inclination of the human heart is evil from youth; nor will I ever again destroy every living creature as I have done.
[22]   As long as the earth endures,
>   seedtime and harvest, cold and heat,
> summer and winter, day and night,
>   shall not cease."

A pause for meditation & prayer upon the scripture . . .

Another Voice　　Julian of Norwich (1342–1416)

I saw that God is everything that is good and energizing.

God is our clothing
that wraps, clasps and encloses us
so as to never leave us.

God showed me in my palm
a little thing round as a ball
about the size of a hazelnut.
I looked at it with the eye of my
understanding and asked myself:
"What is this thing?"

And I was answered: "It is everything that
is created."

I wondered how it could survive since
it seemed so little it could suddenly
disintegrate into nothing.
The answer came: "It endures and ever will
endure, because God loves it."

And so everything has being
because of God's love.

Prayer　　Ray Simpson, Community of Aidan and Hilda

We give you thanks
Because earth's life and fruitfulness flow from you
And all times and seasons reflect your laws.
We give you thanks
Because you created the world in love
You redeemed the world through love
You maintain the world by your love.
Help us to give our love to you.

Blessing   "All Shall Be Well"   Daniel J. McGill

All shall be well
    The seasons echo in their passing.
All shall be well
    The birds promise in their migration.
All shall be well
    The young promise in their growing.
All shall be well
    The old promise in their contentment.
All shall be well
    Sunset promises in its splendor.
All shall be well
    The Sun promises in the morning.
All shall be well
    The storms promise in their moisture.
All shall be well
    The Christ promises in his rising.
All shall be well.

Wednesday

Wisdom: Creation Teaches

MORNING

Opening   Psalm 24:1 (BARNETT)

The world and everything in it belongs
to the Holy One,
so too the fertile world and all
who live there.

Hymn   "All Things Bright and Beautiful"   Cecil Frances Alexander, 1848

Refrain:
All things bright and beautiful,
All creatures great and small,
All things wise and wonderful:
The Lord God made them all.

Each little flower that opens,
Each little bird that sings:
God made their glowing colors,
God made their tiny wings.

The purple-headed mountain,
The river running by,
The sunset, and the morning
That brightens up the sky,

The cold wind in the winter,
The pleasant summer sun,
The ripe fruits in the garden:
God made them every one.

God gave us eyes to see them,
And lips that we might tell
How great is God Almighty,
Who has made all things well.

Scripture   Proverbs 30:18-19, 24-28 (GNT)

[18]   There are four things that are too mysterious
            for me to understand:
[19]   an eagle flying in the sky,
            a snake moving on a rock,
            a ship finding its way over the sea,
            and a man and a woman falling in love.

[24]   There are four animals in the world that are small,
            but very, very clever:
[25]   Ants: they are weak,
            but they store up their food in the summer.
[26]   Rock badgers: they are not strong either,
            but they make their homes among the rocks.
[27]   Locusts: they have no king,
            but they move in formation.
[28]   Lizards: you can hold one in your hand,
            but you can find them in palaces.

A pause for meditation & prayer upon the scripture . . .

Other Voices   Christina Rossetti (1830–94)

The tiniest living thing
That soars on feathered wing,
Or crawls among the long grass out of sight,
Has just as good a right
To its appointed portion of delight
As any King.

Thomas à Kempis (c. 1379–1471)

If your heart be right, then every created thing will become for you a
mirror of life and a book of holy teaching. For there is nothing created
so small and mean that it does not reflect the goodness of God.

Prayer   Gail A. Ricciuti

For all things bright and beautiful,
For all things dark and mysterious and lovely,
For all things green and growing and strong,
For all things weak and struggling to push life up through rocky earth,

For all human faces, hearts, minds, and hands which surround us,
And for all nonhuman minds and hearts, paws and claws,
    fins and wings,
For this Life and the life of this world,
For all that you have laid before us, O God,
We lay our thankful hearts before you. In Christ's name,
    Amen.

Blessing   *with apologies to Cole Porter*

Ants do it; bees do it;
even earthworms in the ground do it.
May you also do it:
be the you
in joyful fullness
in whom God delights.

MIDDAY

Reflection   William Carlos Williams (1883–1963)

There is nothing to eat,
  seek it where you will,
    but the body of the Lord.
The blessed plants
  and the sea, yield it
    to the imagination
intact.

Prayer

From you and of you
is everything that nourishes
my seeing, hearing, tasting, smelling, touching.
As you yield yourself to me
in and through your creation,
let me yield myself to you
wholly.

[handwritten annotation: God shows u what He is like in creation. "Seek His face." Found in creation in the seasons...]

EVENING

Opening   Psalm 90:1-2 (NJB)

Lord, you have been our refuge
from age to age.
Before the mountains were born,
before the earth and the world came to birth,
from eternity to eternity you are God.

Scripture   Ecclesiastes 3:1-11 (NRSV)

[1]   For everything there is a season, and a time for every matter
      under heaven:
[2]   a time to be born, and a time to die;
          a time to plant, and a time to pluck up what is planted;
[3]   a time to kill, and a time to heal;
          a time to break down, and a time to build up;
[4]   a time to weep, and a time to laugh;
          a time to mourn, and a time to dance;
[5]   a time to throw away stones, and a time to gather stones together;
          a time to embrace, and a time to refrain from embracing;
[6]   a time to seek, and a time to lose;
          a time to keep, and a time to throw away;
[7]   a time to tear, and a time to sew;
          a time to keep silence, and a time to speak;
[8]   a time to love, and a time to hate;
          a time for war, and a time for peace.
[9]   What gain have the workers from their toil?
[10] I have seen the business that God has given to everyone to be
busy with. [11] He has made everything suitable for its time;
moreover he has put a sense of past and future into their minds, yet
they cannot find out what God has done from the beginning to the end.

A pause for meditation & prayer upon the scripture . . .

Another Voice   Rachel Carson (1907–1964)

To stand at the edge of the sea, to sense the ebb and the flow of the tides, to feel the breath of a mist moving over a great salt marsh, to watch the flight of shore birds that have swept up and down the surf lines of the continents for untold thousands of years, to see the running of the old eels and the young shad to the sea, is to have knowledge of things that are as nearly eternal as any earthly life can be.

Prayer   Metropolitan Tryphon, 1934

Glory to you,
showing your unfathomable might in the
laws of the universe!
Glory to you,
for all nature is permeated by your laws,
Glory to you
for what you have revealed to us in your goodness,
Glory to you
for all that remains hidden from us in your wisdom,
Glory to you
for the inventiveness of the human mind,
Glory to you
for the invigorating effort of work,
Glory to you
for the tongues of fire which bring inspiration,
Glory to you,
O God, from age to age.

Blessing

Day and night, waking and sleeping,
all times are in God's hands.
May you rest tonight
in the gentle palm of Jesus.

Thursday

Humankind's Vocation

MORNING

Opening   Psalm 143:8 (REB)

In the morning let me know of your love,
for I put my trust in you.
Show me the way that I must take,
for my heart is set on you.

Hymn   "O How Glorious, Full of Wonder"   Curtis Beach, 1958,
rev. 1980; alt.

O how glorious, full of wonder
is your name o'er all the earth,
God, who wrought creation's splendor,
bringing suns and stars to birth!
Rapt in reverence we adore you,
marveling at your mystic ways.
Humbly now we bow before you,
lifting up our hearts in praise.

When we see your lights of heaven,
moon and stars, your power displayed,
Who are we that you should love us,
creatures that your hand has made?
Born of earth, yet full of yearning,
mixture strange of good and ill,
From your ways so often turning,
yet your love does seek us still.

You have set us in communion
with the wonders of your hand,
Made us fly with eagle pinion,
pilgrims over sea and land.
Soaring spire and ruined city,

these our hopes and failures show.
Teach us more of human pity,
that we in your image grow.

O how wondrous, O how glorious
is your name in every land,
God, whose purpose shines before us
toward the goal that you have planned!
Yours the will our hearts are seeking,
conscious of our human need.
Spirit in our spirit speaking, make us yours,
O God, indeed.

Scripture   Psalm 8 (NAB)

[2] O Lord, our Lord,
        how awesome is your name through all the earth!
        You have set your majesty above the heavens!
[3] Out of the mouths of babes and infants
        you have drawn a defense against your foes,
        to silence enemy and avenger.
[4] When I see your heavens, the work of your fingers,
        the moon and the stars that you set in place—
[5] What are humans that you are mindful of them,
        mere mortals that you care for them?
[6] Yet you have made them little less than a god,
        crowned them with glory and honor.
[7] You have given them rule over the works of your hands,
        put all things at their feet:
[8] All sheep and oxen,
        even the beasts of the field,
[9] the birds of the air, the fish of the sea,
        and whatever swims the paths of the seas.
[10] O Lord, our Lord,
        how awesome is your name through all the earth!

A pause for meditation & prayer with the scripture . . .

Other Voices   Beatrice of Nazareth (c. 1200–1268)

> As the fish swims freely
> in the vastness of the seas,
> as the bird soars boldly
> in the vastness of the air,
> so I feel my spirit roaming free
> in the depths and heights and immensity
> of love.

Karl Barth (1886–1968)

Of all creatures the Christian is the one who not merely is a creature, but actually says Yes to being a creature.

Prayer   Isidore of Seville (c. 560–636)

> O God, great and wonderful,
> who has created the heavens,
> dwelling in their light and beauty;
> who has made the earth,
> revealing yourself in every flower that opens.
> Let not my eyes be blind to you,
> neither let my heart be dead,
> but teach me to praise you,
> even as the lark which offers her song at daybreak.

Blessing

> May you experience anew
> God's great Yes to you and to creation—
> and may this Yes set you free
> to live and love abundantly.

The way today's society
is set up puts more
barriers between us and God
buildings, lack of communication
God is found in nature and others
— if those aren't there
God can be elusive

MIDDAY

Reflection   Fyodor Dostoyevsky (1821–81)
from *The Brothers Karamazov*

Love all God's creation,
the whole and every grain of sand in it.
Love every leaf,
every ray of God's light.
Love the animals,
love the plants,
love everything.
If you love everything,
you will perceive
the divine mystery in things.
Once you perceive it,
you will begin to comprehend it better every day.
And you will come at last to love the whole world
with an all-embracing love.

Prayer

Help me, dear God,
to see my brother with the eyes of Christ,
to hear my sister with the ears of Christ,
to taste my neighbor's hunger with the mouth of Christ,
to smell creation's beauty with the nose of Christ,
to touch the world's pain with the hands of Christ
and to love life, each life, every life,
with the heart of Christ.

Evening

Opening   Psalm 16:7 (GRAIL)

> I will bless you, Lord, you give me counsel,
> and even at night direct my heart.

Scripture   Philippians 4:4-9 (NRSV)

[4] Rejoice in the Lord always; again I will say, Rejoice. [5] Let your gentleness be known to everyone. The Lord is near. [6] Do not worry about anything, but in everything by prayer and supplication with thanksgiving let your requests be made known to God. [7] And the peace of God, which surpasses all understanding, will guard your hearts and your minds in Christ Jesus.

[8] Finally, beloved, whatever is true, whatever is honorable, whatever is just, whatever is pure, whatever is pleasing, whatever is commendable, if there is any excellence and if there is anything worthy of praise, think about these things. [9] Keep on doing the things that you have learned and received and heard and seen in me, and the God of peace will be with you.

A pause for meditation & prayer upon the scripture . . .

Another Voice   Hildegard of Bingen (1098–1179)

> When I open my eyes,
> my God, on all that you have created
> I have heaven already in my hands.
>
> Serenely I gather in my lap
> roses and lilies and all green things
> while I praise your works.
>
> My own works I ascribe entirely to you.
> Gladness springs forth from sorrow,
> and joy brings happiness.

Prayer

Thank you for the ways
in which you have opened my eyes this day
to see the heaven of your nearness—
in the true and the honorable,
the just and the pure.
Let all who are weary
find rest tonight,
and let us rise up tomorrow
secure in your peace.

Blessing   Iona Community

Bless to us, O God,
the moon that is above us,
the earth that is beneath us,
the friends who are around us,
your image deep within us,
Amen.

Friday
Sin and the Destruction of Creation

MORNING

Opening   Lancelot Andrewes (1555–1626)

> Essence beyond essence, Nature uncreate,
> Framer of the world,
> I set you, Lord, before my face,
> and I lift up my soul to you.
>
> I worship you on my knees,
> and humble myself under your mighty hand.

Hymn   "Healing River"   Fran Minkoff, 1964

O healing river, send down your waters,
Send down your waters upon this land.
O healing river, send down your waters,
And wash the blood from off the sand.

This land is parching, this land is burning,
No seed is growing in the barren ground.
O healing river, send down your waters,
O healing river, send your waters down.

Let the seed of freedom, awake and flourish,
Let the deep roots nourish,
let the tall stalks rise.
O healing river, send down your waters,
O healing river, from out of the skies.

Scripture   Jeremiah 4:22-26 (NRSV)

[22] "My people are foolish,
         they do not know me;
      they are stupid children,
         they have no understanding.

> They are skilled in doing evil,
>> but do not know how to do good."

[23] I looked on the earth, and lo, it was waste and void;
>> and to the heavens, and they had no light.

[24] I looked on the mountains, and lo, they were quaking,
>> and all the hills moved to and fro.

[25] I looked, and lo, there was no one at all,
>> and all the birds of the air had fled.

[26] I looked, and lo, the fruitful land was a desert,
>> and all its cities were laid in ruins
>> before the LORD, before his fierce anger.

A pause for meditation & prayer upon the scripture . . .

Other Voices   Ronald A. Simkins

Environmental abuse knows no race, creed, or gender. The human species is the only common denominator.

Kate Compston

> How
> can we sing a new song from
> the valley of shards?
> We are broken vessels
> in a fissured land, indeed
> we can hear
> the parchment earth crack open
> beneath our feet even
> as we speak.

> What
> can we do *except*
> sing songs of protest, lamentation, hope
> from split and bleeding lips
> in the valley of splintered dreams?
> What, except believe
> that earth, like a fragile egg
> cracks open to expose
> new quiverings of life?

Prayer   Iona Community

There is no pain in our hearts or in our planet
that you do not know,
for you have touched the lowest places on earth.

Teach us to grieve with you, O Christ,
the loss of all the beauty that is being killed.

There is no place in the heavens
that cannot be touched by your resurrection presence,
for you fill all things.

Give us strength in your victory over death
to grow into your way of love,
which does not despair but keeps sowing seeds of hope
and making signs of wholeness.

Under Christ's control
all the different parts of the body fit together
and the whole body is held together
by every joint with which it is provided.

Teach us to know our interconnectedness with all things.
Teach us to grow with each other
and all living creatures through love.

Blessing   Norman C. Habel

May the life-giving power
  of Jesus Christ's body and blood
  flow through your veins,
  flow through your lives,
  and flow through this Earth.
May this life-giving power
  bring healing and hope
  wherever there are wounds,
  and brokenness.
Go in peace,
  and serve your God,
    each other,
      and all creation.
        Amen.

MIDDAY

Reflection   David W. Orr

Overflowing landfills, befouled skies, eroded soils, polluted rivers, acidic rain, and radioactive wastes suggest ample attainments for admission into some intergalactic school for learning-disabled species.

Prayer

Help me to accept responsibility for my sin:
the ways in which I abuse your creation;
my role, both active and passive,
in marring your image
in myself, other people,
and the earth.
Help me also to accept your forgiveness,
learn from my mistakes,
and live more wisely.

EVENING

Opening   Daniel J. McGill

Give ear to your creation, O God;
for your name's sake deliver it;
And as your light is filling the heavens,
may our hands turn back from evil
and bring delight upon the Earth.

Scripture   Isaiah 33:7-10 (MESSAGE)

But look! Listen!
  Tough men weep openly.
  Peacemaking diplomats are in bitter tears.
The roads are empty—
  not a soul out on the streets.
The peace treaty is broken,

its conditions violated,
    its signers reviled.
The very ground under our feet mourns,
    the Lebanon mountains hang their heads,
Flowering Sharon is a weed-choked gully,
    and the forests of Bashan and Carmel? Bare branches.

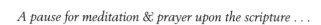

"Now I'm stepping in," GOD says.
    "From now on, I'm taking over.
    The gloves come off. Now see how mighty I am."

A pause for meditation & prayer upon the scripture . . .

Another Voice   World Council of Churches

The destruction of the environment cries out for urgent
repentance and conversion. We are beckoned to rediscover a
biblical vision and a new understanding of ourselves and God's
creation. The only future foreshadowed by the present crises,
both social and ecological, is massive suffering, both human
and other than human. "Giver of Life—Sustain your Creation!"
is our prayer; we should pray it without ceasing.

Prayer   The Anglican Church in Aotearoa, New Zealand and Polynesia

Creator, we disfigure your world.
Lord, have mercy.
Lord, have mercy.

Redeemer, we reject your redemption and crucify you daily.
Christ, have mercy.
Christ, have mercy.

Giver of life, we too often choose death.
Lord, have mercy.
Lord, have mercy.

Blessing   *based on* Psalm 37:3

> May you settle down and be at peace,
> trusting in God's goodness.

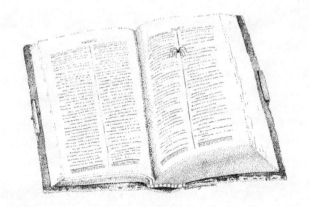

Saturday
God's Recreation

MORNING

Opening   *based on* Isaiah 43:1

But now says the Holy One,
the one who created you, O Jacob,
the one who formed you, O Israel:
"Do not be afraid, for I have redeemed you;
I have called you by name, you are mine."

Hymn   "Christ, Whose Glory Fills the Skies"   Charles Wesley, 1740

Christ, whose glory fills the skies,
Christ, the true, the only light,
Sun of Righteousness, arise,
Triumph o'er the shades of night;
Dayspring from on high, be near;
Daystar, in my heart appear.

Scripture   2 Corinthians 5:17-18 (NRSV)

[17] So if anyone is in Christ, there is a new creation: everything old has passed away; see, everything has become new! [18] All this is from God, who reconciled us to himself through Christ, and has given us the ministry of reconciliation.

A pause for meditation & prayer upon the scripture . . .

Other Voices   Sallie McFague

In prayer a reversal occurs:
we do not talk about God and the world
but begin to see ourselves and the world in God.
We begin to see human life and the world

from the divine perspective,
from a broader and more inclusive point of view
than we are otherwise capable of holding.
We begin to recognize who we are in the scheme of things
from the perspective of the Creator and Redeemer of everything that is.
We are no longer the center (a definition of sin);
we know God is the Center (a definition of salvation).

Marga Bührig (1915–2002)

What can I do for justice, peace, creation?
To learn a new love for life,
my life, part of creation,
related to everything that lives and moves.
To let myself be challenged
when I see around me human destruction of the world.
To break through the veil of deception
that hides from my eyes brutal facts.
And to resist wherever I can,
with subversive power.

Prayer   Jürgen Moltmann

God, Father, Son and Holy Spirit,
triune God,
unite with yourself your torn and divided world,
and let us all be one in you,
one with your whole creation,
which praises and glorifies you

What does being one mean to you?

and in you is happy.
Amen.

Blessing

Today, in Christ,
you are a new creation.
Today, in Christ,
the creation itself is made new.
With Christ's own courage and compassion,
may you begin your new life
in this new creation
today.

MIDDAY

Reflection   Rainer Maria Rilke (1875–1926)

> All will come again into its strength:
> the fields undivided, the waters undammed,
> the trees towering and the walls built low.
> And in the valleys, people as strong
> and varied as the land.
>
> And no churches where God
> is imprisoned and lamented
> like a trapped and wounded animal.
> The houses welcoming all who knock
> and a sense of boundless offering
> in all relations, and in you and me.
>
> No yearning for an afterlife, no looking beyond,
> no belittling of death,
> but only longing for what belongs to us
> and serving earth, lest we remain unused.

Prayer

> Into your stength, this day,
> let me come again—
> my heart undivided, my hope undimmed.
> Set free my soul, unbind my love,
> that I may serve you
> serving earth.

EVENING

Opening   Psalm 85:11-12 (NAB)

> Love and truth will meet;
>   justice and peace will kiss.
> Truth will spring from the earth;
>   justice will look down from heaven.

Scripture   Hosea 2:18-20 (NRSV)

[18] I will make for you a covenant on that day with the wild animals, the birds of the air, and the creeping things of the ground; and I will abolish the bow, the sword, and war from the land; and I will make you lie down in safety. [19] And I will take you for my wife forever; I will take you for my wife in righteousness and in justice, in steadfast love, and in mercy. [20] I will take you for my wife in faithfulness; and you shall know the LORD.

A pause for meditation & prayer upon the scripture . . .

Another Voice   U.N. Environmental Sabbath Program

We join with the earth and with each other.

To bring new life to the land
To restore the waters
To refresh the air

We join with the earth and with each other.

To renew the forests
To care for the plants
To protect the creatures

We join with the earth and with each other.

To celebrate the seas
To rejoice in the sunlight
To sing the song of the stars

We join with the earth and with each other.

To recreate the human community
To promote justice and peace
To remember our children of the earth

We join with the earth and with each other.

We join together as many and diverse expressions of
    one loving mystery: for the healing of the
    earth and the renewal of all life.

Prayer   Anne Rowthorn

> Blessed are you,
> God of growth and discovery;
> yours is the inspiration
> that has altered and changed our lives;
> yours is the power that has brought us
> to new dangers and opportunities.
> Guide us in your holy creation,
> to walk through this world,
> watching and learning,
> loving and trusting,
> until the coming of your reign. Amen.

Blessing   *based on* Hosea 14:7

> May you rest beneath God's shade,
> flourish like a garden,
> blossom like a vine;
> and your soul become as fragrant
> as the finest wine.

Peace
Leave a fragrance
— when some people
leave — stench

Sunday

Sabbath: The Praise of Creation

MORNING

Opening   Psalm 98:7-8 (NRSV)

> Let the sea roar, and all that fills it;
>> the world and those who live in it.
> Let the floods clap their hands;
>> let the hills sing together for joy.

Hymn   "O That I Had a Thousand Voices"   Johann Mentzer, 1704
Trans. *The Lutheran Hymnal*, 1941; alt.

> All creatures that have breath and motion,
> That throng the earth, the sea, the sky,
> Come, share with me my heart's devotion,
> Help me to sing God's praises high!
> My utmost powers can never quite
> Declare the wonders of God's might!

Scripture   Psalm 148 (SCHRECK & LEACH)

[1]   Praise God from the heavens;
     praise God in the heights;
[2]   praise God, all you angels;
     praise God, all you heavenly hosts.

[3]   Praise God, sun and moon;
     praise God, all you shining stars.
[4]   Praise God, you highest heavens,
     and you waters above the heavens.

[5]   Let them praise the name of God,
     who commanded and they were created.
[6]   God established them forever and ever
     and gave a decree that shall not pass away.

[7]   Praise God all the earth,
      you sea monsters and all depths,
[8]   fire and hail, snow and mist,
      storm winds that fulfill God's word.
[9]   You mountains and all you hills,
      you fruit trees and all you cedars,
[10] you wild beasts and all tame animals,
      you creeping things and flying birds.

[11] Let the rulers of the earth and all peoples
      and all the judges of the earth—
[12] young men too, and maidens,
      old women and men—
[13] praise the name of God
      whose name alone is exalted;
      whose majesty is above earth and heaven,
      and who has raised the fortunes of the people.

[14] Be this God praised by all the faithful ones,
      by the children of Israel, the people close to God.
      Alleluia.

A pause for meditation & prayer upon the scripture . . .

Another Voice   Euros Bowen (1904–1988)   Trans. by C. Davies

YR HOLL FYD SY'N LLAWN GOGONIANT:

The whole world is full of glory.

Here is the glory of created things,
   the earth and the sky,
      the sun and the moon,
         the stars and the vast expanses:

Here is fellowship
   with all that was created,
      the air and the wind,
         cloud and rain,
               sunshine and snow:

All life like the bubbling of a flowing river
   and the dark currents of the depths of the sea
                        is full of glory.

Prayer   Anon. Welsh, ed. by Oliver Davies and Fiona Bowie

Hail to you, glorious Lord!
May church and chancel praise you,
May chancel and church praise you,
May plain and hillside praise you,
May the three springs praise you,
Two higher than the wind and one above the earth,
May darkness and light praise you,
May the cedar and the sweet fruit-tree praise you.
Abraham praised you, the founder of faith,
May life everlasting praise you,
May the birds and beasts praise you
May the stubble and the grass praise you.
Aaron and Moses praised you,
May male and female praise you,
May the seven days and the stars praise you,
May the lower and upper air praise you,
May books and letters praise you,
May the sand and the earth praise you,
May all good things created praise you,
And I too shall praise you, Lord of glory,
Hail to you, glorious Lord.

Blessing   *based on* Genesis 49:25-26

May God Almighty bless you.
Blessings of heavens above,
    blessings of the deep lying below,
        blessings of the breasts and the womb,
            blessings of the grain and the flowers,
                blessings of the eternal mountains,
                    bounty of the everlasting hills,
                        be with you and go with you.
                            Amen.

MIDDAY

Reflection   Iris Murdoch (1919–99)

People from a planet without flowers would think we must be mad with joy the whole time to have such things about us.

Prayer

Drive me mad with joy, O God,
to have your grace surround me
everywhere, everyday
in such ordinary,
superbly natural
things.

EVENING

Opening   *based on* Isaiah 61:10

I sing my joy to the Lord,
my whole body thrills with delight—
for God has dressed me
in robes of justice and salvation,
like a groom with his garland
or a bride with her jewels.

Scripture   Song of Solomon 2:8-13 (NRSV)

[8]   The voice of my beloved!
           Look, he comes,
       leaping upon the mountains,
           bounding over the hills.
[9]   My beloved is like a gazelle
           or a young stag.
       Look, there he stands
           behind our wall,

gazing in at the windows,
   looking through the lattice.
[10] My beloved speaks and says to me:
   "Arise, my love, my fair one,
     and come away;
[11] for now the winter is past,
   the rain is over and gone.
[12] The flowers appear on the earth;
   the time of singing has come,
  and the voice of the turtledove
   is heard in our land.
[13] The fig tree puts forth its figs,
   and the vines are in blossom;
   they give forth fragrance.
  Arise, my love, my fair one,
  and come away."

A pause for meditation & prayer upon the scripture . . .

Another Voice   Gertrud the Great of Helfta (1256–1301/1302)

[D]uring that day when you are at leisure for love (for the kindling of your senses by the true sun, who is God, so that your love may never be extinguished but may grow from day to day) assiduously reflect on one of these verses:

   Blessed the eyes that see you, O God, love. . . .
   Blessed are the ears that hear you, O God, love, Word of life. . . .
   Blessed the nose that breathes you, O God, love, life's most dulcet
     aroma. . . .
   Blessed the mouth that tastes, O God, love, the words of your
     consolation, sweeter than honey and the honeycomb. . . .
   Blessed the soul that clings inseparably to you in an embrace of
     love and
   blessed the heart that senses the kiss of your heart, O God, love.

Prayer

God our Lover:
through the extravagance of creation
you arouse my love for you,
and I am seduced by your grace.

Awaken me,
body, mind, and spirit,
to the glory of your seduction
in earth and sky and water,
flower and tree and bird,
eye and ear and skin.

Blessing   *based on* Song of Solomon 8:6-7

May Christ set you as a seal upon his heart,
as a seal upon his arm;
for his love is as strong as death,
his passion as fierce as the grave.
Many waters cannot quench his love,
neither can floods drown it.

WEEK
THREE

Monday

Beginnings

MORNING

Opening   *based on* Psalm 36:9

> You are the fount of life, O God:
> You give us light,
> and we see.

Hymn   "This Little Light of Mine"   African-American Spiritual

> This little light of mine, I'm goin' to let it shine.
> This little light of mine, I'm goin' to let it shine.
> This little light of mine, I'm goin' to let it shine.
>   Let it shine, let it shine, let it shine.
>
> Everywhere I go, I'm goin' to let it shine . . .
>
> All through the night, I'm goin' to let it shine . . .

Scripture   Genesis 1:14-19 (NRSV)

[14] And God said, "Let there be lights in the dome of the sky to separate the day from the night; and let them be for signs and for seasons and for days and years, [15] and let them be lights in the dome of the sky to give light upon the earth." And it was so. [16] God made the two great lights—the greater light to rule the day and the lesser light to rule the night—and the stars. [17] God set them in the dome of the sky to give light upon the earth, [18] to rule over the day and over the night, and to separate the light from the darkness. And God saw that it was good. [19] And there was evening and there was morning, the fourth day.

A pause for meditation & prayer upon the scripture . . .

Another Voice   Francis of Assisi (1182–1226)

> Such love does
> the sky now pour,
> that whenever I stand in a field,
>
> I have to wring out the light
> when I get
> home.

Prayer   Matins Prayer, Armenian Sunrise Office

From the East to the West,
from the North and the South,
all nations and peoples
bless the creator of creatures with a new blessing.

· ·

O congregations of the righteous,
    who glorify the Holy Trinity in the morning of light,
praise the Christ, the morning of peace,
together with the Father and the Spirit;
    for he has made the light of his knowledge
    shine over us.

Blessing

May Christ open your eyes
that you may see the light of creation.
May Christ open your ears
that you may hear the song of the earth.
May Christ open your heart
that you may give and receive love.

MIDDAY

Reflection   U.S. Astronaut James Irwin (1930–91)

From the moon the earth looked just like a marble, the most beautiful
marble you can imagine. The earth is uncommonly lovely. It is the only
warm living object that we saw in space on our flight to the moon. . . .

That beautiful, warm living object looked so fragile, so delicate, that if you touched it with a finger it would crumble and fall apart. Seeing this has to change a man, has to make a man appreciate the creation of God and the love of God.

Prayer

> Creator Spirit:
> As the earth,
> so beautiful, so warm,
> receives and reflects the sunlight,
> so may I receive and reflect your love.

EVENING

Opening   *based on* 1 John 1:5; 2:10

Our God is light,
and in God there is no darkness.
Whoever loves,
lives in this light.

Scripture   2 Corinthians 4:5-6 (NRSV)

[5] For we do not proclaim ourselves; we proclaim Jesus Christ as Lord and ourselves as your slaves for Jesus' sake. [6] For it is the God who said, "Let light shine out of darkness," who has shone in our hearts to give the light of the knowledge of the glory of God in the face of Jesus Christ.

A pause for meditation & prayer upon the scripture . . .

Another Voice   Iona Community

We believe in a bright and amazing God,
who has been to the depths of despair
on our behalf;
who has risen in splendour and majesty;
who decorates the universe

with sparkling water, clear white light,
twinkling stars and sharp colours,
over and over again.

> We believe that Jesus is the light of the world;
> that God believes in us, and trusts us,
> even though we make the same mistakes
> over and over again.

> > We commit ourselves
> > to Jesus,
> > to one another as brothers and sisters,
> > and to the Maker's business in the world.

> > > God said: Let there be light.
> > > Amen.

God trusts me even when I don't trust myself. Amy sqi't I trust

Prayer   Presbyterian Church (U.S.A.)

As you have made this day, O God,
you also make the night.
Give light for our comfort.
Come upon us with quietness and still our souls
that we may listen for the whisper of your Spirit
and be attentive to your nearness in our dreams.
Empower us to rise again in new life
to proclaim your praise,
and show Christ to the world. Amen.

Blessing

> The light of Christ
> shines even in the darkness.
> May you rest this night
> in the gentle warmth of his light.

Tuesday

God's Providence: Continuing Creation

MORNING

Opening   Psalm 89:6*a*,12 (NAB)

The heavens praise your marvels, LORD. . . .
Yours are the heavens, yours the earth;
    you founded the world and everything in it.

Hymn   "Great Is Thy Faithfulness"   Thomas O. Chisholm, 1923

Great is Thy faithfulness, O God my Father,
There is no shadow of turning with Thee;
Thou changest not, Thy compassions they fail not;
As Thou hast been Thou forever wilt be.

Refrain:
Great is Thy faithfulness! Great is Thy faithfulness!
Morning by morning new mercies I see;
All I have needed Thy hand hath provided;
Great is Thy faithfulness, Lord, unto me!

Summer and winter, and springtime and harvest,
Sun, moon, and stars in their courses above
Join with all nature in manifold witness
To Thy great faithfulness, mercy, and love.
Refrain

Scripture   Matthew 6:25-33 (NRSV)

[25] "Therefore I tell you, do not worry about your life, what you will eat or what you will drink, or about your body, what you will wear. Is

not life more than food, and the body more than clothing? [26] Look at the birds of the air; they neither sow nor reap nor gather into barns, and yet your heavenly Father feeds them. Are you not of more value than they? [27] And can any of you by worrying add a single hour to your span of life? [28] And why do you worry about clothing? Consider the lilies of the field, how they grow; they neither toil nor spin, [29] yet I tell you, even Solomon in all his glory was not clothed like one of these. [30] But if God so clothes the grass of the field, which is alive today and tomorrow is thrown into the oven, will he not much more clothe you—you of little faith? [31] Therefore do not worry, saying, 'What will we eat?' or 'What will we drink?' or 'What will we wear?' [32] For it is the Gentiles who strive for all these things; and indeed your heavenly Father knows that you need all these things. [33] But strive first for the kingdom of God and his righteousness, and all these things will be given to you as well."

A pause for meditation & prayer upon the scripture . . .

Another Voice   Catherine of Siena (1347–80)

How can people see me feeding and nurturing the worm within the dry wood, pasturing the brute beasts, nourishing the fish in the sea, all the animals on the earth and the birds in the air, commanding the sun to shine on the plants and the dew to fertilize the soil, and not believe that I nourish them as well, my creatures made in my image and likeness? As a matter of fact, all this is done by my goodness to serve them. No matter where they turn, spiritually and materially they will find nothing but my deep burning charity and the greatest, gentle, true, perfect providence.

Prayer

Lord Jesus,
may I trust the faithfulness of your Father
who feathers and feeds the birds.
In the people I meet,
the places I go,
the food that I eat,
help me to see and hear,
taste and touch
the abundance of your grace
within the landscape of your love.

> Set me free from anxiety
> and the burden of excess
> so that I may share with others
> the gifts I have received.

Blessing   Edmund Banyard

> Holy is the soil we walk on,
> Holy everything that grows,
> Holy all beneath the surface,
> Holy every stream that flows.

MIDDAY

Reflection   "The Avowal"   Denise Levertov (1923–97)

> As swimmers dare
> to lie face to the sky
> and water bears them,
> as hawks rest upon air
> and air sustains them,
> so would I learn to attain
> freefall, and float
> into Creator Spirit's deep embrace,
> knowing no effort earns
> that all-surrounding grace.

Prayer

> Into your arms, loving Lord, let me "freefall,"
> upheld by your goodness and mercy.
> Secure in your embrace,
> show me how to love without effort,
> trust without fear,
> and live with abandon.

EVENING

Opening   Psalm 95:6-7 (NAB)

Enter, let us bow down in worship;
   let us kneel before the LORD who made us.
For this is our God,
   whose people we are,
   God's well-tended flock.

Scripture   Psalm 23 (NAB)

[1]   The LORD is my shepherd;
      there is nothing I lack.
[2]   In green pastures you let me graze;
      to safe waters you lead me;
[3]   you restore my strength.
      You guide me along the right path
      for the sake of your name.
[4]   Even when I walk through a dark valley,
      I fear no harm for you are at my side;
      your rod and staff give me courage.

[5]   You set a table before me
      as my enemies watch;
      You anoint my head with oil;
      my cup overflows.
[6]   Only goodness and love will pursue me
      all the days of my life;
      I will dwell in the house of the LORD
      for years to come.

A pause for meditation & prayer upon the scripture . . .

Another Voice   Henry David Thoreau (1817–62)

We may live the life of a plant or an animal
without living an animal life.
This constant and universal content of the animal
comes of resting quietly in God's palm.
I feel as if I could at any time resign my life

notoun and the responsibility into God's hands,
and become as innocent and free from care as a plant or stone.

Prayer   Metropolitan Tryphon, 1934

I was born a weak, defenceless child, but your angel, spreading his radiant wings, guarded my cradle. From my birth, your love has illumined my paths, and has wondrously guided me towards the light of eternity. From my first day until now, the generous gifts of your providence have been wonderfully showered upon me. I give you thanks, and with all those who have come to know you, I exclaim:

Glory to you for calling me into being,
Glory to you for spreading out before me the beauty of the universe,
Glory to you for revealing to me through heaven and earth
   the eternal book of wisdom,
Glory to your eternity within this fleeting world,
Glory to you for your mercies, seen and unseen,
Glory to you for every sigh of my sorrow,
Glory to you for every step in my life's journey,
   for every moment of joy,
Glory to you, O God, from age to age.

Blessing

Sleep tonight
knowing that you—
and all of creation—
are secure in the arms
of our Shepherd.

Wonderful prayer

Wednesday

Wisdom: Creation Teaches

MORNING

Opening   Psalm 84:4 (GRAIL)

The sparrow herself finds a home
and the swallow a nest for her brood;
she lays her young by your altars,
Lord of hosts, my king and my God.

Hymn   *from* "There's a Wideness in God's Mercy"   Frederick W. Faber, 1854

There's a wideness in God's mercy like the wideness of the sea;
there's a kindness in God's justice, which is more than liberty.

For the love of God is broader than the measure of our mind;
and the heart of the Eternal is most wonderfully kind.

If our love were but more simple, we should rest upon God's word;
and our lives would be illumined by the presence of our Lord.

Scripture   Job 12:7-10 (NRSV)

[7]   "But ask the animals, and they will teach you;
   the birds of the air, and they will tell you;
[8]   ask the plants of the earth, and they will teach you;
   and the fish of the sea will declare to you.
[9]   Who among all these does not know
   that the hand of the LORD has done this?
[10]   In his hand is the life of every living thing
   and the breath of every human being."

A pause for meditation & prayer upon the scripture . . .

Another Voice   "On Fly-Fishing"   Richard D. Adams (1939–2005)

There is the pressure of water on your legs as you wade the stream.
There are all the subtle smells—
the aroma of water itself
and then the smell of the emerging trees and shrubs.
Then come the sounds:
the birdsong and occasional drumming of a grouse,
and sometimes the call of a turkey.
Added to this is the sound of the wind in the pine branches.
Finally there are the sights.
The glint of sun on the water—
a thousand dancing diamonds. . . .
Somehow when you are in the water,
animals don't recognize you as a person.
You wade past deer lying along a bank
without spooking them.
You can touch their nose with the end of your rod. . . .
But nature is not tame.
My Pennsylvania woods are populated
with two varieties of poisonous snakes.
That adds a dimension of danger.
I suspect that God is not tame
or entirely safe.

Prayer   Attributed to Albert Schweitzer (1875–1965)

Hear our humble prayer, O God,
for our friends the animals,
especially for animals who are suffering;
for any that are hunted or lost or deserted or frightened or hungry;
for all that must be put to death.
We entreat for them all thy mercy and pity
and for those who deal with them
we ask a heart of compassion,
gentle hands and kindly words.
Make us ourselves to be true friends to animals
and so to share the blessing of the merciful.

Blessing

May you experience today
both the wideness and the wildness
of God's grace—
in sun and sky,
wind and water,
animal and plant,
and in the drumming
of your own heart.

MIDDAY

Reflection   Holmes Rolston III

Wildness is a bizarre place where our conventional values get
   roughed up.
We learn the relativity and subjectivity
   of what in civilization can seem such basic rules.
Wild nature doesn't know my frames of reference
   and can't in the slightest care about my deepest cultural norms.
In wildness there is no time of day;
   it is not 10:00 a.m. Eastern Daylight Time,
   nor is it Tuesday or July.
There are no board-feet, BTUs, meters, miles;
the lines of latitude and longitude and elevation contours do not
   really exist.
There is no English or German, no literature or conversation.
The numbers and words are gone,
   and we know them for the cultural improvisations
   and mathematical overlays they are.
One leaves money in the car and enters a different economy. . . .
In wildness there is neither capitalism nor socialism,
   neither democracy nor monarchy, science nor religion.
There is no honesty, justice, mercy, or duty. . . .

So what, if anything, is positively of value there?
There is light and dark, life and death.
There is time almost everlasting
   and a genetic language two billion years old.

There is energy and evolution inventing fertility and prowess,
    adaptation and improvisation, information and strategy,
    contest and compliance, display and flair.
There is muscle and fat, nerve and sweat,
    law and form, structure and process, beauty and cleverness,
    harmony and sublimity, tragedy and glory.

Prayer

Untamed Spirit:
Rough up my "conventional values"
with the wildness of your love and creativity.
Help me to let go
of my need to predict and control
and let me enter
the unmapped regions
of your grace.

EVENING

Opening   Lutheran World Federation

Spirit of the wind and the whirlwind,
breathing through every person and place,
    open our eyes to the mysteries of creation,
    as you did with Job long long ago.

Scripture   Job 38:1-7 (NRSV)

[1]   Then the LORD answered Job out of the whirlwind:
[2]   "Who is this that darkens counsel by words without knowledge?
[3]   Gird up your loins like a man,
       I will question you, and you shall declare to me.

[4]   "Where were you when I laid the foundation of the earth?
       Tell me, if you have understanding.
[5]   Who determined its measurements—surely you know!
       Or who stretched the line upon it?
[6]   On what were its bases sunk,
       or who laid its cornerstone

[7]   when the morning stars sang together
       and all the heavenly beings shouted for joy?"

A pause for meditation & prayer upon the scripture . . .

Another Voice   Bill McKibben

The facts—the testimony of the psalmist, the evidence of our own
eyes and ears, the emerging understanding of the atmospheric
chemists—lead to the same conclusions that God draws for Job in his
mighty speech. Our anthropocentric bias is swept away. The question
becomes this: what will replace it?

    Humility, first and foremost. That is certainly Job's reaction. If we
are not, as we currently believe, at the absolute epicenter of the
created world, then we need to learn to humble ourselves.

Prayer

    You are God—not me, not us;
    help me to remember this simple fact each day.
    You are the Center of creation—not me, not us;
    help me to recognize my place within the orbit of your grace.
    You are the Source of all life—not me, not us;
    let me find in you my kinship with all creation.

Blessing   *based on* Deuteronomy 31:6

    Be strong and of good courage;
    do not fear—for God goes with you;
    and God will never fail, forget, or forsake you.

Thursday

Humankind's Vocation

MORNING

Opening   *based on* Matthew 25:40

Jesus said:
"I tell you solemnly,
Whatever you did to the least of these,
You did to me."

Hymn   "Touch the Earth Lightly"   Shirley Erena Murray, 1992

Touch the earth lightly, use the earth gently,
nourish the life of the world in our care:
Gift of great wonder, ours to surrender,
trust for the children tomorrow will bear.

. . . .

Let there be greening, birth from the burning,
water that blesses, and air that is sweet,
Health in God's garden, hope in God's children,
regeneration that peace will complete.

God of all living, God of all loving,
God of the seedling, the snow, and the sun,
Teach us, deflect us, Christ reconnect us,
using us gently, and making us one.

Scripture   Wisdom of Solomon 9:1-3, 4a (NRSV)

[1]   "O God of my ancestors and Lord of mercy,
         who have made all things by your word,
[2]   and by your wisdom have formed humankind
         to have dominion over the creatures you have made,

[3]   and rule the world in holiness and righteousness,
          and pronounce judgment in uprightness of soul. . . .
[4]   give me the wisdom that sits by your throne.

Another Voice   John Woolman (1720–72)

[I] was early convinced in my mind that true religion consisted in an inward life, wherein the heart doth love and reverence God the Creator and learn to exercise true justice and goodness, not only towards all men but also towards the brute creatures; that as the mind was moved on an inward principle to love God as an invisible, incomprehensible being, on the same principle it was moved to love him in all his manifestations in the visible world; that as by his breath the flame of life was kindled in all animal and sensitive creatures, to say we love God as unseen and at the same time exercise cruelty towards the least creature moving by his life, or by life derived from him, was a contradiction in itself.

Prayer   Christian Conference of Asia, 1991

Creator God, breathing your own life into
    being,
you gave us the gift of life:
you placed us on this earth
    with its minerals and waters,
    flowers and fruits,
    living creatures of grace and beauty.
You gave us the care of the earth.

. . . .

Teach us, Creator God of Love,
That the earth and all its fullness is yours,
The world and all who dwell in it.
Call us yet again to safeguard the gift of life.
Amen.

Blessing

Safeguarded by the Spirit,
may you grow more just and compassionate
in your relationship to the earth, other people,
your own self,
and the God who is within and beyond the totality of life.

MIDDAY

Reflection   Carl Sagan (1934–96)

One picture that I very much wanted to take—which we finally were able to take—was a picture of the Earth from the outskirts of the solar system. And there it was, a single pixel, or a single picture element, a pale blue dot. No continents, no national boundaries, no beings, no humans, just a dot. That's us. That's where we live. That's where everyone we know, everyone we love, everyone we ever heard of, every human being who ever lived has lived: on that pale blue dot. Every hopeful child, every couple in love, every prince and pauper, every revered religious leader, every corrupt politician, every scientist, every humble person living out his or her days—all of us—every one of us and all the other beings, live on that pale blue dot.

To me it underscores our responsibility, because you look at that dot and you think how fragile and vulnerable it is. Our central responsibility is to cherish and care for the environment on the only home we have ever known and the only home for all those other beings with whom we are so profoundly connected.

Prayer

Against the dark backdrop of infinite space,
    our planet appears so small, so vulnerable.
Guide me, dear God,
    that I may cherish your earth
        and the life it sustains
            with the best of my energy,
                intelligence, imagination,
                    and love.

EVENING

Opening   Psalm 16:7-8 (BARNETT)

I bless you, Holy One. You guide me,
    and nightly instruct my inner being.

I set you always before me;
    with you at my right hand,
I cannot fall.

Scripture   Micah 6:6-8 (NRSV)

[6]   "With what shall I come before the LORD,
        and bow myself before God on high?
    Shall I come before him with burnt offerings,
        with calves a year old?
[7]   Will the LORD be pleased with thousands of rams,
        with ten thousands of rivers of oil?
    Shall I give my firstborn for my transgression,
        the fruit of my body for the sin of my soul?"
[8]   He has told you, O mortal, what is good;
        and what does the LORD require of you
    but to do justice, and to love kindness,
        and to walk humbly with your God?

A pause for meditation & prayer upon the scripture . . .

Other Voices   John Chrysostom (c. 347–407)

Holy people are most loving and gentle in their dealings with their
fellows, and even with the lower animals: for this reason it was said
that "A righteous man is merciful to the life of his beast."
    Surely we ought to show kindness and gentleness to animals
for many reasons and chiefly because they are of the same origin
as ourselves.

Leonardo Boff

That is good which conserves and promotes all creatures, especially living creatures, and among living beings, the weakest; that which is bad is
everything that prejudices, debases, and destroys living creatures.

Prayer   Jane Austen (1775–1817)

Incline us oh God! to think humbly of ourselves,
    to be severe only in the examination of our own conduct,
    to consider our fellow-creatures with kindness,
    and to judge of all they say and do with that charity
    which we would desire from them ourselves.

Blessing

May the great, vulnerable, life-giving Spirit
guide your every coming and your every going,
that you may act justly,
love kindly,
and walk humbly
as God's friend and companion
on this lovely, lively planet.

Friday

Sin and the Destruction of Creation

MORNING

Opening   Psalm 85:12-13 (BARNETT)

Holy One, you will indeed grant prosperity
   and our land will yield her harvests.
True justice goes before you
   and prepares a pathway for your footsteps.

Hymn   "We Cannot Own the Sunlit Sky"   Ruth Duck, 1984; rev. 1989

We cannot own the sunlit sky, the moon, the wildflowers growing,
for we are part of all that is within life's river flowing.
With open hands receive and share the gifts of God's creation,
that all may have abundant life in every earthly nation.

When bodies shiver in the night and, weary, wait for morning,
when children have no bread but tears, and warhorns sound
      their warning,
God calls humanity to wake, to join in common labor,
that all may have abundant life in oneness with their neighbor.

God calls humanity to join as partners in creating
a future free from want or fear, life's goodness celebrating.
That new world beckons from afar, invites our shared endeavor,
that all may have abundant life and peace endure forever.

Scripture   Deuteronomy 11:13-17 (NRSV)

[13] If you will only heed his every commandment that I am commanding you today—loving the LORD your God, and serving him with all your
heart and with all your soul—[14] then he will give the rain for your
land in its season, the early rain and the later rain, and you will gather in
your grain, your wine, and your oil; [15] and he will give grass in your

fields for your livestock, and you will eat your fill. [16] Take care, or you will be seduced into turning away, serving other gods and worshiping them, [17] for then the anger of the LORD will be kindled against you and he will shut up the heavens, so that there will be no rain and the land will yield no fruit; then you will perish quickly off the good land that the LORD is giving you.

A pause for meditation & prayer upon the scripture . . .

Another Voice   Presbyterian Church in Taiwan

We believe that God has given human beings dignity,
talents and a homeland, so that they may share in God's creation,
and have responsibility with Him for taking care of the world.
Therefore, they have social, political and economic systems, arts
and sciences, and a spirit which seeks after the true God.
But humans beings have sinned, and they misuse these gifts,
destroying the relationship between themselves, all creatures, and God.
Therefore, they must depend on the saving grace of Jesus Christ.
He will deliver humankind from sin, will set the oppressed free
and make them equal, that all may become new creatures in
Christ, and the world His Kingdom, full of justice, peace and joy.

Prayer   U.N. Environmental Sabbath

Gracious God,
who made the covenant promise with our ancestors,
we gather here today a rebellious people.
We want to act out your intentions for us,
but we keep getting mixed up
by all the glitter of the world around us.
You tell us to honor creation,
and we use other people and animals and plant life
only to meet our wants.
You offer daily bread to every living creature,
and we steal that bread from our brothers and sisters
in the name of our greed.
You promise us new life,
and we shrink back from it in fear.
Heal us, God, lest we destroy ourselves.
We need your presence among us. Amen.

Blessing

> Forgiven and set free by the risen Christ,
> may his life flow through you—
> body, mind, and spirit—
> so that you may be an agent of life,
> life abundant,
> here, in this place,
> now, in this day.

MIDDAY

Reflection   Donella H. Meadows (1941–2001)

Very deep

This fresh apple, still cold and crisp from the morning dew, is not-me only until I eat it. When I eat, I eat the soil that nourished the apple. When I drink, the waters of the earth become me. With every breath I take in I draw in not-me and make it me. With every breath out, I exhale me into not-me.

If the air and the waters and the soils are poisoned, I am poisoned. Only if I believe the fiction of the lines more than the truth of the line-less planet will I poison the earth, which is myself.

Prayer

> Erase all the lines, O God,
> that I have drawn in my mind
> to separate the life that is "not-me"
> from the life that is "me."
> Enlarge the boundaries of my heart
> to include soil and water,
> air and animals,
> friend and stranger—
> all that, in Christ, you've called me
> to love and nourish.

EVENING

Opening   John 10:10 (NRSV)

[Jesus said:]
"I came that they may have life,
and have it abundantly."

Scripture   Hosea 4:1-3 (NRSV)

[1]   Hear the word of the LORD, O people of Israel;
    for the LORD has an indictment against the
        inhabitants of the land.
    There is no faithfulness or loyalty,
      and no knowledge of God in the land.
[2]   Swearing, lying, and murder,
    and stealing and adultery break out;
    bloodshed follows bloodshed.
[3]   Therefore the land mourns,
    and all who live in it languish;
  together with the wild animals
    and the birds of the air,
    even the fish of the sea are perishing.

A pause for meditation & prayer upon the scripture . . .

Another Voice   Janet Morley

Let us name what is evil in our world,
and in the name of Jesus proclaim its defeat.

In a world where the rich are protected
from understanding the lives of the poor,
let us believe the words of Jesus:
I have seen Satan fall.

In a world where the demands of international debt
are more important than the health of children,
let us believe the words of Jesus:
I have seen Satan fall.

In a world where unjust laws and practices
privilege white people over others,
let us believe the words of Jesus:
I have seen Satan fall.

In a world where women are silenced and exploited
let us believe the words of Jesus:
I have seen Satan fall.

In a world where the lives of ordinary workers
are violated by the military,
let us believe the words of Jesus:
I have seen Satan fall.

In a world where the earth and its forests
are plundered and destroyed,
let us believe the words of Jesus:
I have seen Satan fall.

Prayer   "The Millennium Resolution"   Churches Together in England

Let there be
respect for the earth
peace for its people
love in our lives
delight in the good
forgiveness for past wrongs
and from now on a new start.

Blessing

In your sleeping, in your waking,
you are cherished by the God who made you.
May you arise tomorrow
ready to live the love you have received
and to cherish the life of creation.

Saturday

God's Recreation

MORNING

Opening   *based on* Ephesians 1:8b-10

With all wisdom and grace
God has revealed the mystery
of what is intended:
a plan for the fullness of time
to unite the universe through Christ.

Hymn   "Sing Praise to God, Who Reigns Above"
Johann Jacob Schütz, 1675; trans. Frances Elizabeth Cox, 1864; alt.

Sing praise to God, who reigns above,
The God of all creation,
The God of power, the God of love,
The God of our salvation;
With healing balm my soul is filled,
And every faithless murmur stilled:
To God all praise and glory!

Scripture   Isaiah 11:6-9 (NRSV)

Will everything and everyone be vegetarian?

[6]   The wolf shall live with the lamb,
the leopard shall lie down with the kid,
the calf and the lion and the fatling together,
and a little child shall lead them.
[7]   The cow and the bear shall graze, *Do bears graze?*
their young shall lie down together;
and the lion shall eat straw like the ox.
[8]   The nursing child shall play over the hole of the asp,
and the weaned child shall put its hand on the adder's den.
[9]   They will not hurt or destroy on all my holy mountain;
for the earth will be full of the knowledge of the LORD
as the waters cover the sea.

A pause for meditation & prayer upon the scripture . . .

Another Voice   Denis Edwards

It is no more difficult to believe in God's power at work in the resurrection of one person than it is to believe in the transformation of the universe.

Prayer   The Royal Society for the Prevention of Cruelty to Animals

Holy Father,
your Son, Jesus Christ
is the reconciler of all things
in heaven and on earth;
send us your Spirit
that we may be made one
with all your creatures,
and know that all things
come from you,
through you,
and belong to you
now and forever.

Blessing

May you go out today in peace,
believing in God's power to transform all creation,
including you.

MIDDAY

Reflection   Philip Ball

Every day, every passing second, water is on the move. The rivers flow, the oceans perform their slow and elegant gyrations, the clouds congeal and weep. Each 3100 years, a volume of water equivalent to all the oceans passes through the atmosphere, carried there by evaporation and removed by precipitation. . . . This constant overturn of water between the reservoirs on land, in sea, and in sky is called the hydrological cycle,

and it is as crucial for life on Earth as is the presence of liquid water in
the first place.

Prayer

Every day, every passing second,
your grace, like water, is on the move—
bringing new life,
baptizing your creation.
> Immersed in your Spirit,
> may I move within the cycle
> of your love,
> giving my life, like water,
> to any who thirst.

EVENING

Opening   Isaiah 55:12 (NRSV)

For you shall go out in joy,
> and be led back in peace;
the mountains and the hills before you
> shall burst into song,
> and all the trees of the field shall clap their hands.

Scripture   Colossians 1:15-20 (NAB)

[15] [Christ] is the image of the invisible God,
> the firstborn of all creation.
[16] For in him were created all things in heaven and on earth,
> the visible and the invisible,
> whether thrones or dominions or principalities or powers;
> all things were created through him and for him.
[17] He is before all things,
> and in him all things hold together.
[18] He is the head of the body, the church.
> He is the beginning, the firstborn from the dead,
> that in all things he himself might be preeminent.
[19] For in him all the fullness was pleased to dwell,

[20] and through him to reconcile all things for him,
    making peace by the blood of his cross
    [through him], whether those on earth or those in heaven.

A pause for meditation & prayer upon the scripture . . .

Another Voice   Zephania Kameeta

The church does not walk her way in silence or "neutrality," but she
sings with a clear voice the song of victory and liberation. A hymn
that shakes the evil powers and pulls down all destructive schemes
and ideologies. A hymn that lifts up the oppressed, poor and despised
people from the dust and brings down the proud and mighty from
their thrones. A hymn that calls the whole universe to Jesus Christ.

Prayer   Andrew Linzey

    Holy God
    you alone
    can make all things new;
    send your Holy Spirit
    upon us;
    give us new hearts to feel,
    new ears to hear,
    new eyes to see
    the unity of
    all creatures
    in Christ;
    and to proclaim
    all living beings
    as fellow creatures
    with us in your
    wonderful creation.
    Amen.

Blessing   Daniel J. McGill

    God was pleased to reconcile to himself all things,
    whether on Earth or in Heaven.
        **—May we be reconciled to all things
        on Earth and
        in Heaven as well.**

Sunday

Sabbath: The Praise of Creation

MORNING

Sabbath

Opening   Psalm 103:22 (NAB)

Bless the LORD, all creatures,
  everywhere in God's domain.
Bless the LORD, my soul!

Hymn   "From All That Dwell Below the Skies"   Isaac Watts, 1719

From all that dwell below the skies
Let the Creator's praise arise:
Alleluia! Alleluia!
Let the Redeemer's name be sung
Through every land, in every tongue.
Alleluia! Alleluia! Alleluia!
Alleluia! Alleluia!

In every land begin the song,
To every land the strains belong:
Alleluia! Alleluia!
In cheerful sound all voices raise
And fill the world with joyful praise.
Alleluia! Alleluia! Alleluia!
Alleluia! Alleluia!

Eternal are Thy mercies, Lord;
Eternal truth attends Thy word:
Alleluia! Alleluia!
Thy praise shall sound from shore to shore,
Till suns shall rise and set no more.
Alleluia! Alleluia! Alleluia!
Alleluia! Alleluia!

Scripture Exodus 20:8-11 (NRSV)

[8] Remember the sabbath day, and keep it holy. [9] Six days you shall labor and do all your work. [10] But the seventh day is a sabbath to the LORD your God; you shall not do any work—you, your son or your daughter, your male or female slave, your livestock, or the alien resident in your towns. [11] For in six days the LORD made heaven and earth, the sea, and all that is in them, but rested the seventh day; therefore the LORD blessed the sabbath day and consecrated it. *God commands that we rest*

A pause for meditation & prayer upon the scripture . . .

Another Voice Wayne Muller

In the trance of overwork, we take everything for granted. We consume things, people, and information. We do not have time to savor this life, nor to care deeply and gently for ourselves, our loved ones, or our world; rather, with increasingly dizzying haste, we use them all up, and throw them away. . . . *We consume people?*

Sabbath time can be a revolutionary challenge to the violence of overwork, mindless accumulation, and the endless multiplication of desires, responsibilities, and accomplishments. Sabbath is a way of being in time where we remember who we are, remember what we know, and taste the gifts of spirit and eternity.

Prayer

Grant me grace this day
to rest and remember
that there is nothing I have to do,
nothing I have to buy or sell,
nothing I have to produce or consume
in order to become who I already am:
your beloved creation.
  May your overworked creation
  and those who cannot rest today
  come to know the liberation of your sabbath.

Blessing   Early Scottish

> Deep peace of the running wave to you,
> Deep peace of the flowing air to you,
> Deep peace of the quiet earth to you,
> Deep peace of the shining stars to you,
> Deep peace of the Son of Peace to you, for ever.

MIDDAY

Reflection   "Auguries of Innocence"   William Blake (1757–1827)

> To see a World in a grain of sand,
> And a Heaven in a wild flower,
> Hold Infinity in the palm of your hand,
> And Eternity in an hour. . . .

Prayer

> May I see today
> the largeness of your love
> in even the smallest part of creation.
> May I be ravished
> by traces of your beauty
> in earth and sky.
> May I experience
> the eternity of your grace
> pulsing within each moment.

EVENING

Opening   Isaiah 6:3*b* (NRSV)

"Holy, holy, holy is the LORD of hosts;
the whole earth is full of his glory."

Scripture   Daniel 3:74-83 (NJB)

[74] Let the earth bless the Lord:
         praise and glorify him for ever!
[75] Bless the Lord, mountains and hills,
         praise and glorify him for ever!
[76] Bless the Lord, every plant that grows,
         praise and glorify him for ever!
[77] Bless the Lord, springs of water,
         praise and glorify him for ever!
[78] Bless the Lord, seas and rivers,
         praise and glorify him for ever!
[79] Bless the Lord, whales, and everything that
            moves in the waters,
         praise and glorify him for ever!
[80] Bless the Lord, every kind of bird,
         praise and glorify him for ever!
[81] Bless the Lord, all animals wild and tame,
         praise and glorify him for ever!
[82] Bless the Lord, all the human race:
         praise and glorify him for ever!
[83] Bless the Lord, O Israel,
         praise and glorify him for ever!

A pause for meditation & prayer upon the scripture . . .

Another Voice   Scott Hoezee

Perhaps in God's ears, all of this world's sounds really are songs of praise—and what a chorus it is! Some time ago an ornithologist observed a single red-eyed vireo singing its song 22,197 times in a single day! Conservative estimates say that in North America alone there are as many as six billion land birds. So let us be conservative and say that on a given day in the season of spring—the time of the year when birds tend to sing the most—

each of these birds sings its song about ten thousand times. That would be, in North America alone, sixty trillion songs in just one day. "Day after day they pour forth speech." Indeed they do, and God is listening.

Prayer   "Canticle of Creation"   Francis of Assisi (1182–1226)
Trans. by Mary Low

Most high, almighty, good Lord,
to you belong praise and glory and honour
and every blessing.

To you alone do they belong, O Most High
for no one is worthy to pronounce your name.

Praise to you, Lord, through all your creatures,
and especially through our noble Brother Sun,
through whom we have daylight and illumination
for he is beautiful and radiant and dazzling
and he reveals to us something of yourself.

Praise to you, Lord, through Sister Moon and the stars
which you have set in the heavens,
bright and precious and beautiful.

Praise to you, Lord, through Brother Wind
and air and clouds and stillness and every kind of weather
by which you uphold creation.

Praise to you, Lord, through Sister Water
who is very useful and humble and precious and pure.

Praise to you, Lord, through Brother Fire
through whom you light up the darkness
for he is beautiful and cheery and vigorous and mighty.

Praise to you, Lord, for Sister Earth, our mother
who feeds us and governs us
and produces all kinds of fruits and colourful flowers and herbs.

Praise to you, Lord, for all who forgive each other through your love,
and who endure illness and tribulation.
Blessed are they who endure it peaceably
for you will honour them, O Most High.

Praise to you, Lord, for our Sister Death
for no living being can escape from her.
Wretched are they who die in mortal sin.
Blessed are they who are found doing your will
for the second death will not harm them.
Praise and bless my Lord and give thanks to him
and serve him with great humility.

Blessing

As the moon traces its light across the surface of water,
as star-fire pricks the blanket of night,
so may God's love and light
shine in your heart and in your dreaming.

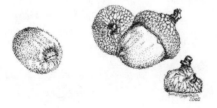

WEEK
FOUR

Monday

Beginnings

MORNING

Opening   Psalm 22:10-11 (GRAIL)

> Yes, it was you who took me from the womb,
> entrusted me to my mother's breast.
> To you I was committed from my birth,
> from my mother's womb you have been my God.

Hymn   *from* "Have Thine Own Way, Lord"   Adelaide A. Pollard, 1901

> Have thine own way, Lord! Have thine own way!
> Thou art the potter, I am the clay.
> Mold me and make me after thy will,
> while I am waiting, yielded and still.
>
> Have thine own way, Lord! Have thine own way!
> Hold o'er my being absolute sway.
> Fill with thy Spirit till all shall see
> Christ only, always, living in me.

Scripture   Psalm 139:13-18 (NRSV)

[13] For it was you who formed my inward parts;
> you knit me together in my mother's womb.
[14] I praise you, for I am fearfully and wonderfully made.
> Wonderful are your works;
> that I know very well.
[15] My frame was not hidden from you,
> when I was being made in secret,
> intricately woven in the depths of the earth.
[16] Your eyes beheld my unformed substance.
> In your book were written
> all the days that were formed for me,
> when none of them as yet existed.

[17] How weighty to me are your thoughts, O God!
How vast is the sum of them!
[18] I try to count them—they are more than the sand;
I come to the end—I am still with you.

A pause for meditation & prayer upon the scripture . . .

Another Voice   John Calvin (1509–1564)

When we examine [the human body], even to the nails of our fingers,
there is nothing which could be altered, without felt inconveniency. . . .
Where is the embroiderer who, with all his industry and ingenuity, could
execute the hundredth part of this complicated and diversified struc-
ture? We need not then wonder if God, who formed man so perfectly
in the womb, should have an exact knowledge of him after he is ush-
ered into the world.

Prayer   Janet Morley

God of wholeness,
you have created us bodily,
that our work and faith may be one.
May we offer our worship
from lives of integrity;
and maintain the fabric of this world
with hearts that are set on you,
through Jesus Christ, Amen.

Blessing

The God who weaves the sun and the moon,
the sky and the earth,
is the very same God who knit you together
in your mother's womb.
The God who brings new stars to birth in far-off galaxies
is the same God who brought you to birth and
placed you at your mother's breast.

Enter this day with confidence:
as surely as the sun,
as certain as the moon,
as solid as the earth,
you have a place within God's unfolding grace.

MIDDAY

Reflection   Pattiann Rogers

"Watching the Ancestral Prayers of Venerable Others"

Lena Higgins, 92, breastless,
blind, chewing her gums by the window,
is old, but the Great Comet of 1843

is much older than that. Dry land
tortoises with their elephantine
feet are often very old, but giant

sequoias of the western Sierras
are generations older than that.
The first prayer rattle, made

on the savannah of seeds and bones
strung together, is old, but the first
winged cockroach to appear on earth

is hundreds of millions of years
older than that. A flowering plant
fossil or a mollusk fossil in limy
shale is old. Stony meteorites buried
beneath polar ice are older than that,
and death itself is very, very

ancient, but life is certainly older
than death. Shadows and silhouettes
created by primordial sea storms

erupting in crests high above
one another occurred eons ago,
but the sun and its flaring eruptions

existed long before they did. Light
from the most distant known quasar
seen at this moment tonight is old

(should light be said to exist
in time), but the moment witnessed
just previous is older than that.

The compact, pea-drop power
of the initial, beginning nothing
is surely oldest, but then the intention,

with its integrity, must have come
before and thus is obviously
older than that. Amen.

Prayer

You:
from the first, and before.
You:
the farthest future, and after.
You:
the now, this moment, the eternal present.
Your grace, time's arrow;
your love, life's integrity.
Amen.

EVENING

Opening   *based on* Ephesians 1:4

Before time, before creation,
God chose us in Christ
to live a pure and holy life,
full of love.

Scripture   Hebrews 11:1-3 (NRSV)

[1] Now faith is the assurance of things hoped for, the conviction of things not seen. [2] Indeed, by faith our ancestors received approval. [3] By faith we understand that the worlds were prepared by the word of God, so that what is seen was made from things that are not visible.

A pause for meditation & prayer upon the scripture . . .

Another Voice   Moyra Caldecott

Our being is the expression of God's Thought.
We contain the love of God and God contains us
and as we unfold on earth
through shell-creature,
fish-form,
reptile,
bird,
and mammal—
through ichthyosaurs
plesiosaurs
dinosaurs
and ape—
we are learning
step by step
what that containment means.

The circles are still widening—
still evolving the mighty concept—
the magnificent Idea.
Six days,
Seven . . .
a million years,
a thousand million . . .
the count is nothing,
the Being—All.
Praise be to our great God
and the Word that resonates
in our hearts still.

May we not separate ourselves in arrogance
from the Great Work
for we know the sound of the Word
but not its full meaning.

Prayer   John McQuiston II

Incomprehensible Mystery,
Here in this instant and always,
Deep within our being,
From the dust of stars
You brought us into existence,

And provided this day.
From the moment of birth,
You have sheltered us from death.
As night falls,
Help us, in your grace,
To be thankful,
And to make our lives worthy of your gifts.
Amen.

Blessing

Since the beginning,
when God first prepared the worlds,
laying the foundations of life,
you have been known and loved by God.
Rest and sleep tonight,
completely known,
securely loved.

Tuesday

God's Providence: Continuing Creation

MORNING

Opening   Psalm 108:4-5 (NAB)

I will praise you among the peoples, LORD;
   I will chant your praise among the nations.
For your love towers to the heavens;
   your faithfulness, to the skies.

Hymn   "We Plow the Fields and Scatter"   Matthias Claudius, 1782
Trans. Jane Montgomery Campbell, 1861; alt.

We plow the fields and scatter
The good seed on the land,
But it is fed and watered
By God's almighty hand;
God sends the snow in winter,
The warmth to swell the grain,
The breezes and the sunshine,
And soft, refreshing rain.

You only are the Maker
Of all things near and far;
You paint the wayside flower,
You light the evening star;
The winds and waves obey You,
By You the birds are fed;
Much more to us, Your children,
You give our daily bread.

Scripture   Joel 2:21-24 (NRSV)

[21] Do not fear, O soil; be glad and rejoice,
         for the LORD has done great things!
[22] Do not fear, you animals of the field,
         for the pastures of the wilderness are green;
      the tree bears its fruit,
         the fig tree and vine give their full yield.
[23] O children of Zion, be glad
         and rejoice in the LORD your God;
      for he has given the early rain for your vindication,
         he has poured down for you abundant rain,
         the early and the later rain, as before.
[24] The threshing floors shall be full of grain,
         the vats shall overflow with wine and oil.

A pause for meditation & prayer upon the scripture . . .

Another Voice   Hildegard of Bingen (1098–1179)

I, the fiery life of divine wisdom,
I ignite the beauty of the plains,
I sparkle the waters,
I burn in the sun,
      and the moon,
      and the stars.

With wisdom I order ALL rightly.
. . . .

I adorn all the earth.

I am the breeze
that nurtures all things green.
. . . .

I am the rain
coming from the dew
that causes the grasses to laugh
with the joy of life.

I call forth tears,
the aroma of holy work.
I am the yearning for good.

Prayer   Chief Dan George (1899–1981)

The beauty of the trees,
the softness of the air,
the fragrance of the grass,
    speaks to me.

The summit of the mountain,
the thunder of the sky,
the rhythm of the sea,
    speaks to me.

The faintness of the stars,
the freshness of the morning,
the dew drop on the flower,
    speaks to me.

The strength of fire,
the taste of salmon,
the trail of the sun,
And the life that never goes away,
    They speak to me.

And my heart soars.

Blessing

May God
who gardens the galaxies,
fueling star-fire,
watering the world,
greening the earth—
    May this God
    guide you
    guard you
    and give you growth.

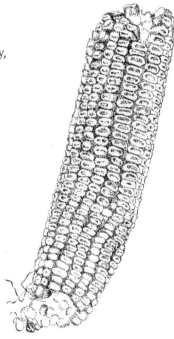

MIDDAY

Reflection and Prayer   Thomas Traherne (1637–74)

Let all Thy creatures bless Thee O Lord,
and my soul praise and bless Thee for them all.
I give Thee thanks for the being
Thou givest unto the heavens, sun, moon, stars, and elements;
to beasts, plants, and all other bodies of the earth;
to the fowls of the air, the fishes of the sea.
I give Thee thanks for the beauty of colours,
for the harmony of sounds,
for the pleasantness of odours,
for the sweetness of meats,
for the warmth and softness of our raiment,
and for all my five senses,
and all the pores of my body,
so curiously made . . . ,
and for the preservation as well as use
of all my limbs and senses. . . .
Above all, I praise Thee for manifesting Thyself unto me,
whereby I am made capable of praise
and magnify Thy name for evermore.

EVENING

Opening   Isaiah 32:15 (NRSV)

A spirit from on high is poured out on us,
and the wilderness becomes a fruitful field,
and the fruitful field is deemed a forest.

Scripture   Psalm 65:5-13 (NRSV)

[5]   By awesome deeds you answer us with deliverance,
O God of our salvation;
you are the hope of all the ends of the earth
and of the farthest seas.

[6]   By your strength you established the mountains;
        you are girded with might.
[7]   You silence the roaring of the seas,
        the roaring of their waves,
        the tumult of the peoples.
[8]   Those who live at earth's farthest bounds are awed by your signs;
        you make the gateways of the morning and the
            evening shout for joy.

[9]   You visit the earth and water it,
        you greatly enrich it;
      the river of God is full of water;
        you provide the people with grain,
        for so you have prepared it.
[10] You water its furrow abundantly,
        settling its ridges, softening it with showers,
        and blessing its growth.
[11] You crown the year with your bounty;
        your wagon tracks overflow with richness.
[12] The pastures of the wilderness overflow,
        the hills gird themselves with joy,
[13] the meadows clothe themselves with flocks,
        the valleys deck themselves with grain,
        they shout and sing together for joy.

A pause for meditation & prayer upon the scripture . . .

Another Voice   Frederick Buechner

Using the same old materials of earth, air, fire, and water, every twenty-four hours God creates something new out of them. If you think you're seeing the same show all over again seven times a week, you're crazy. Every morning you wake up to something that in all eternity never was before and never will be again. And the you that wakes up was never the same before and will never be the same again either.

Prayer   Walter Rauschenbusch (1861–1918)

O God, we thank you for this earth, our home; for the wide sky and the blessed sun, for the salt sea and the running water, for the everlasting hills and the never-resting winds, for trees and the common grass underfoot.

We thank you for our senses by which we hear the songs of birds, and see the splendour of the summer fields, and taste of the autumn fruits, and rejoice in the feel of the snow, and smell the breath of the spring.

Grant us a heart wide open to all this beauty; and save our souls from being so blind that we pass unseeing when even the common thorn-bush is aflame with your glory, O God our creator, who lives and reigns for ever and ever.

Blessing   Ray Simpson, Community of Aidan and Hilda

> Peace to the land and all that grows on it
> Peace to the sea and all that swims in it
> Peace to the air and all that flies through it
> Peace to the night and all who sleep in it.

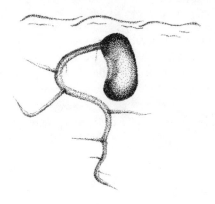

Wednesday

Wisdom: Creation Teaches

MORNING

Opening   Thomas Merton (1915–68), *adapted*

This flower,
this light,
this moment,
this silence:
Dominus est . . .
The flower is itself.
The light is itself.
The silence is itself.
I am myself . . .
We are here in Him.

Hymn   "Christ the Apple Tree"   Anonymous
from a collection of Joshua Smith, New Hampshire, 1784

The tree of life my soul hath seen,
Laden with fruit, and always green:
The trees of nature fruitless be
Compared with Christ the apple tree.

His beauty doth all things excel:
By faith I know, but ne'er can tell
the glory which I now can see
In Jesus Christ the apple tree.

For happiness I long have sought,
And pleasure dearly I have bought:
I missed of all: but now I see
'Tis found in Christ the apple tree.

I'm weary with my former toil,
Here I will sit and rest a while:

Under the shadow I will be
Of Jesus Christ the apple tree.

This fruit doth make my soul to thrive,
It keeps my dying faith alive;
Which makes my soul in haste to be
With Jesus Christ the apple tree.

Scripture   Jeremiah 17:7-8 (NRSV)

[7]   Blessed are those who trust in the LORD,
        whose trust is the LORD.
[8]   They shall be like a tree planted by water,
        sending out its roots by the stream.
    It shall not fear when heat comes,
        and its leaves shall stay green;
    in the year of drought it is not anxious,
        and it does not cease to bear fruit.

A pause for meditation & prayer upon the scripture . . .

Another Voice   Joyce Rupp

Whenever I spend time with a tree there's always a teaching to help me with whatever is calling me to grow. . . .

I've learned how to not be broken from life's unwanted things by watching a willow in the wild wind tossing and bending rather than pushing back against the storm. It's taught me that I can't always have everything go my way. . . .

Paper birches have reminded me to surrender as their bark peeled off to aid the growth. The ponderosa pines of Colorado have urged me to be resilient as they stood sturdily through the turbulent mountain seasons. Enduring cottonwoods, with their many fibrous roots, have counseled me to sink strong webbing roots of love and faith so I will still be nourished in dry times when I question most everyone and everything.

Old dead trees in the moist woods persuaded me that life can come through death as their decaying bodies nurture soil and seeds. The sycamore's round terminal buds on leafless branches showed me how to wait patiently through the dormant times of my inner winters when all seemed unable and unworthy of growth. . . .

A new green shoot growing from a maple stump assured me that new life can come despite my woundedness, and the mighty redwoods have advised me that aging can be a graceful process with an inherent dignity.

On and on the teachings go. They never end. Not as long as I listen to the trees.

Prayer   Joy Cowley

Dear God, there are times
when I hear your voice most clearly
in greenness: in the singing of sap,
the conversations of the leaves, the whisperings
of shoot and stem, root, sap and cell,
calling me back to creation
to feel again the freshness of you
running through everything
like a bright emerald current.

Blessing

Rooted and grounded in the Creator's love,
entwined in Christ's own life,
may you hear the song of the Spirit today
in trees and grass, in forest and field,
and in the tender stretching of your own heart.

MIDDAY

Reflection   Barbara Kingsolver

I'm a scientist who thinks it wise to enter the doors of creation not with a lion tamer's whip and chair, but with the reverence humankind has traditionally summoned for entering places of worship: a temple, a mosque, or a cathedral. A sacred grove, as ancient as time.

Prayer   Charles Cummings, *adapted*

> In the same manner, O Christ,
> that I receive your body and blood—
> let me receive and handle
> the gifts of your creation:
> without waste or abuse,
> but with reverent hands
> and a grateful heart.

EVENING

Opening   Proverbs 3:18 (NRSV)

> [Wisdom] is a tree of life to those who lay hold of her;
>   those who hold her fast are called happy.

Scripture   Psalm 1:1-3 (NAB)

[1]   Happy those who do not follow
           the counsel of the wicked,
       Nor go the way of sinners,
           nor sit in company with scoffers.
[2]   Rather, the law of the LORD is their joy;
           God's law they study day and night.
[3]   They are like a tree
           planted near streams of water,
       that yields its fruit in season;
       Its leaves never wither;
           whatever they do prospers.

A pause for meditation & prayer upon the scripture . . .

Another Voice   Howard Thurman (1899–1981)

When the storms blew, the branches of the large oak tree in our
backyard would snap and fall. But the topmost branches of the oak
tree would sway, giving way just enough to save themselves from
snapping loose. I needed the strength of that tree, and, like it, I wanted

to hold my ground. Eventually, I discovered that the oak tree and I had a unique relationship. I could sit, my back against its trunk, and feel the same peace that would come to me in my bed at night. I could reach down in the quiet places of my spirit, take out my bruises and my joys, unfold them, and talk about them. I could talk aloud to the oak tree and know that I was understood. It, too, was part of my reality, like the woods, the night, and the pounding surf, my earliest companions, giving me space.

Prayer

Tonight and tomorrow
let me stand beside you, O God;
let me sit beneath your branches.
Let your life grow within me
so that my faith may bear fruit
for those who hunger
and my hope provide shade
for those who despair.
As leaves transform sunlight into food,
may Christ's love transform
everything I say and do,
giving life to others.

Blessing

Like roots below the surface, drinking in water—
may you take into your body, your soul,
the life-giving nourishment of sleep,
and sink into the deep rest
of God's peace.

Thursday

Humankind's Vocation

MORNING

Opening   Mark 8:34 (NRSV)

[Jesus said:]
"If any want to become my followers, let them deny themselves
and take up their cross and follow me."

Hymn   *from* "When I Survey the Wondrous Cross"   Isaac Watts, 1707

When I survey the wondrous cross
On which the Prince of glory died,
My richest gain I count but loss,
And pour contempt on all my pride.

Were the whole realm of nature mine,
That were a present far too small;
Love so amazing, so divine,
Demands my soul, my life, my all.

Scripture   Philippians 2:5-11 (NRSV)

[5]   Let the same mind be in you that was in Christ Jesus,
[6]   who, though he was in the form of God,
         did not regard equality with God
         as something to be exploited,
[7]   but emptied himself,
         taking the form of a slave,
         being born in human likeness.
       And being found in human form,
[8]   he humbled himself
         and became obedient to the point of death—
         even death on a cross.

[9]   Therefore God also highly exalted him
           and gave him the name
           that is above every name,
[10] so that at the name of Jesus
           every knee should bend,
           in heaven and on earth and under the earth,
[11] and every tongue should confess
           that Jesus Christ is Lord,
           to the glory of God the Father.

A pause for meditation & prayer upon the scripture . . .

Another Voice   Sallie McFague

Christian discipleship for twenty-first-century
North American Christians
means "cruciform living,"
an alternative notion of the abundant life,
which will involve a philosophy of "enoughness,"
limitations on energy use, and sacrifice for the sake of others.
For us privileged Christians a "cross-shaped" life
will not be primarily what Christ does for us,
but what we can do for others.
We do not need so much to accept Christ's sacrifice
for our sins as we need to repent
of a major sin—our silent complicity
in the impoverishment of others
and the degradation of the planet.
In Charles Birch's pithy statement:
"The rich must live more simply,
so that the poor may simply live."

Prayer   Wang Weifan

When will I learn, O God,
to see poverty as riches,
to see humility as exaltation,
to find plenty in emptiness,
and empty myself,
so that I may be filled
with all of creation?

Blessing

May joy be yours this day
as you lift and carry the cross—
      a cross that is your own,
      a cross freely chosen,
      a cross that brings you to life
      even as it brings life to others
      and healing to creation.

MIDDAY

Reflection   John Muir (1838–1914)

The world, we are told, was made especially for man—a presumption
not supported by all the facts. . . .

   . . . Why should man value himself as more than a small part of
the one great unit of creation? And what creature of all that the Lord
has taken the pains to make is not essential to the completeness of
that unit—the cosmos? The universe would be incomplete without
man; but it would also be incomplete without the
smallest transmicroscopic creature that dwells
beyond our conceitful eyes and knowledge.

   From the dust of the earth, from the
common elementary fund, the Creator has
made *Homo sapiens*. From the same material
[God] has made every other creature, however
noxious and insignificant to us. They are earth-born
companions and our fellow mortals.

Prayer

    Help me, good Lord,
    to accept my kinship
    with all that you have made—
    from the transmicroscopic
    to the most transcendent.
      Just as, in Christ,
      you made yourself vulnerable

by embracing our humanity,
let me open myself
to the joys, the sufferings,
the needs, and delights
of every life.

EVENING

Opening   Psalm 24:3-4 (NRSV)

Who shall ascend the hill of the LORD?
    And who shall stand in his holy place?
Those who have clean hands and pure hearts,
    who do not lift up their souls to what is false,
    and do not swear deceitfully.

Scripture   Psalm 37:1-6 (NAB)

[1]   Do not be provoked by evildoers;
            do not envy those who do wrong.
[2]   Like grass they wither quickly;
            like green plants they wilt away.

[3]   Trust in the LORD and do good
            that you may dwell in the land and live secure.
[4]   Find your delight in the LORD
            who will give you your heart's desire.

[5]   Commit your way to the LORD;
            trust that God will act
[6]   And make your integrity shine like the dawn,
            your vindication like noonday.

            A pause for meditation & prayer upon the scripture . . .

Other Voices   John H. Westerhoff

The spiritual life, as I understand it, is ordinary, everyday life lived in an ever-deepening and loving relationship to God and therefore to one's true or healthy self, all people, and the whole of creation.

Ron Ferguson

To become aware of the sacramental nature of the cosmos;
to be open to the sacramental possibilities of each moment;
to see the face of Christ in every person;
these things are not novel,
but their rediscovery is the beginning of our health.

Prayer   Uniting Church in Australia

Jesus Christ, help us to see
the glory of God in you,
wearing the flesh and blood and clay
we wear every day.
Help us to see the glory, the face of God
around us in all creation. Amen.

Blessing

In Christ
all things are held together
and his grace is the integrity of creation.
May you know yourself held by Christ
who holds all things
together.

Friday

Sin and the Destruction of Creation

MORNING

Opening   Psalm 51:17 (NRSV)

The sacrifice acceptable to God is a broken spirit;
   a broken and contrite heart, O God, you will not despise.

Hymn   "God Folds the Mountains Out of Rock"   Thomas H. Troeger, 1985

God folds the mountains out of rock
And fuses elemental powers
In ores and atoms we unlock
To claim as if their wealth were ours.
From veins of stone we lift up fire,
And too impressed by our own skill
We use the flame that we acquire,
Not thinking of the Maker's will.

Our instruments can probe and sound
The folded mountain's potent core,
But wisdom's ways are never found
Among the lodes of buried ore,
Yet wisdom is the greater need,
And wisdom is the greater source,
For lacking wisdom we proceed
To waste God's other gifts on force.

Lord, grant us what we cannot mine,
What science cannot plumb or chart:
Your wisdom and your truth divine
Enfolded in a faithful heart.
Then we like mountains richly veined
Will be a source of light and flame
Whose energies have been ordained
To glorify the Maker's name.

Scripture   Jeremiah 12:4 (NRSV)

How long will the land mourn,
  and the grass of every field wither?
For the wickedness of those who live in it
  the animals and the birds are swept away,
  and because people said, "[God] is blind to our ways."

A pause for meditation & prayer upon the scripture . . .

*deforestation
strip mining
Virgin
mountains*

Another Voice   Wangari Maathai

Repeated cycles of this abuse to the environment produce poverty, insecurity and desperation. Can we honestly ask God to intervene, or do we write letters to the relevant ministers of government? Do we demonstrate in the streets to register our disappointment with poor governance of natural resources or do we ask the angels in Heaven to do something about it. Do we make the connection between environmental degradation and the problems which communities face every day?

When we make that connection, the God in us will move and energize us. It will guide us from apathy to action, from being observers to doers in the hope that those actions can make a difference.

Prayer   Christian Conference of Asia, 1991

You gave us the care of the earth.
Today you call us:
"Where are you: what have you done?"
(Silence.)

We hide in shame, for we are naked
We violate the earth and plunder it;
We refuse to share the earth's resources;
We seek to own what is not ours, but yours.
Forgive us, Creator God, and reconcile us to your creation.

Teach us, Creator God of Love,
That the earth and all its fullness is yours,
The world and all who dwell in it.
Call us yet again to safeguard the gift of life.
Amen.

Blessing

> May the Spirit of life move you
> from apathy to action,
> from observing to doing,
> from despair to hope.
>> May the Spirit of life bless you
>> with both the pain and the joy of change—
>> the change the world needs,
>> the change for which you pray,
>> the change you are becoming
>>> through Jesus Christ.

MIDDAY

Reflection   Wendell Berry

The world is being destroyed, no doubt about it, by the greed of the rich and powerful. It is also being destroyed by popular demand. There are not enough rich and powerful people to consume the whole world; for that, the rich and powerful need the help of countless ordinary people. We acquiesce in the wastefulness of destructiveness of the national and global economics by acquiescing in the wastefulness and destructiveness of our own households and communities. If conservation is to have a hope of succeeding, then conservationists, while continuing their effort to change public life, are going to have to begin the effort to change private life as well.

Prayer

> Before I condemn the waste and abuse of others,
> let me not be blind, loving God,
> to the waste and destruction
> within my own home,
> within my own soul.
> Give me a heart of humility
> and a commitment to change.

EVENING

Opening   "Lord of the Universe"   Margaret Clarkson, 1973

Lord of the universe, hope of the world,
how your creation cries out for release!
looks for you, longs for you, watches and waits,
prays for your kingdom of justice and peace!

Scripture   Romans 8:18-25 (NRSV)

[18] I consider that the sufferings of this present time are not worth comparing with the glory about to be revealed to us. [19] For the creation waits with eager longing for the revealing of the children of God; [20] for the creation was subjected to futility, not of its own will but by the will of the one who subjected it, [21] in hope that the creation itself will be set free from its bondage to decay and will obtain the freedom of the glory of the children of God. [22] We know that the whole creation has been groaning in labor pains until now; [23] and not only the creation, but we ourselves, who have the first fruits of the Spirit, groan inwardly while we wait for adoption, the redemption of our bodies. [24] For in hope we were saved. Now hope that is seen is not hope. For who hopes for what is seen? [25] But if we hope for what we do not see, we wait for it with patience.

A pause for meditation & prayer upon the scripture . . .

Another Voice   Basil of Caesarea (c. 329–79)

"The earth is the Lord's and the fulness
thereof." O God, enlarge within us the sense
of fellowship with all living things, our
brothers the animals to whom Thou hast
given the earth as their home in common
with us. We remember with shame that in the past
we have exercised the high dominion of man
with ruthless cruelty, so that the voice of the
earth, which should have gone up to Thee in

song, has been a groan of travail. May we
realize that they live, not for us alone, but for
themselves and for Thee, and that they love
the sweetness of life.

Prayer   Rubem Alves

Lord: Help us to see in the groaning of creation
not death throes but birth pangs;
help us to see in suffering a promise for the future,
because it is a cry against the inhumanity of the present.
Help us to glimpse in protest the dawn of justice,
in the Cross the pathway to resurrection,
and in suffering the seeds of joy.

Blessing   James Weldon Johnson, 1921

God of our weary years,
God of our silent tears,
Thou who hast brought us thus far on the way;
Thou who hast by Thy might led us into the light;
Keep us forever in the path, we pray.

Saturday

God's Recreation

MORNING

Opening   Romans 8:38-39 (NRSV)

For I am convinced that neither death nor life, nor angels, nor rulers, nor things present, nor things to come, nor powers, nor height, nor depth, nor anything else in all creation, will be able to separate us from the love of God in Christ Jesus our Lord.

Hymn   "Joyful, Joyful, We Adore Thee"   Henry van Dyke, 1907; alt.

> Joyful, joyful, we adore Thee,
> God of glory, Lord of love;
> Hearts unfold like flowers before Thee,
> Opening to the sun above.
> Melt the clouds of sin and sadness;
> Drive the gloom of doubt away;
> Giver of immortal gladness,
> Fill us with the light of day.

> All Thy works with joy surround Thee,
> Earth and heaven reflect Thy rays,
> Stars and angels sing around Thee,
> Center of unbroken praise.
> Field and forest, vale and mountain,
> Flowery meadow, flashing sea,
> Chanting bird and flowing fountain,
> Call us to rejoice in Thee.

Scripture   Isaiah 43:15, 18-21 (NRSV)

[15] I am the LORD, your Holy One,
       the Creator of Israel, your King.

[18] Do not remember the former things,
    or consider the things of old.
[19] I am about to do a new thing;
    now it springs forth, do you not perceive it?
    I will make a way in the wilderness
    and rivers in the desert.
[20] The wild animals will honor me,
    the jackals and the ostriches;
    for I give water in the wilderness,
    rivers in the desert,
    to give drink to my chosen people,
    the people whom I formed for myself
    so that they might declare my praise.

A pause for meditàtion & prayer upon the scripture . . .

Another Voice   Bede Griffiths (1906–1993)

Christ had to go through death
in order to enter the new world,
the world of communion with God.
    We have to go through death with him,
    both as individuals and as societies.
        It is the only way.
            This is the challenge that faces the world today.
We are passing out of one world,
the world of Western domination.
    Something new is emerging.
        Our patriarchal culture is being challenged at every level.
    It is a moment of trauma, of birth.
        And in these great movements of change
            we can discern the purposes of God and of his Kingdom.

Prayer   The Anglican Church in Aotearoa, New Zealand and Polynesia

Eternal Spirit,
Earth-maker, Pain-bearer, Life-giver,
Source of all that is and that shall be,
Father and Mother of us all,
Loving God, in whom is heaven:

The hallowing of your name echo through the universe!
The way of your justice be followed by the peoples of the world!
Your heavenly will be done by all created beings!
Your commonwealth of peace and freedom
    sustain our hope and come on earth.
With the bread we need for today, feed us.
In the hurts we absorb from one another, forgive us.
In times of temptation and test, strengthen us.
From trials too great to endure, spare us.
From the grip of all that is evil, free us.

For you reign in the glory of the power that is love,
now and for ever. Amen.

Blessing

May the Creator
give you eyes to see
the new creation springing forth—
May Christ
give you ears to hear
the laughter of new life—
May the Spirit
set the feet of your heart
dancing to the rhythm
of resurrection.

MIDDAY

Reflection   "God's Grandeur"   Gerard Manley Hopkins (1844–89)

The world is charged with the grandeur of God.
  It will flame out, like shining from shook foil;
  It gathers to a greatness, like the ooze of oil
Crushed. Why do men then now not reck his rod?
Generations have trod, have trod, have trod;
  And all is seared with trade; bleared, smeared with toil;
  And wears man's smudge and shares man's smell: the soil
Is bare now, nor can foot feel, being shod.

And for all this, nature is never spent;
  There lives the dearest freshness deep down things;
And though the last lights off the black West went
  Oh, morning, at the brown brink eastward, springs—
Because the Holy Ghost over the bent
  World broods with warm breast and with ah! bright wings.

Prayer   Iona Community

O God, for your love for us, warm and brooding,
which has brought us to birth and opened our eyes
to the wonder and beauty of creation,
we give you thanks.

For your love for us, wild and freeing,
which has awakened us to the energy of creation:
to the sap that flows,
the blood that pulses,
the heart that sings,
we give you thanks.

. . . .

O God, we . . . celebrate
that your Holy Spirit is present deep within us,
and at the heart of all life.
Forgive us when we forget your gift of love
made known to us in Jesus,
and draw us into your presence.

EVENING

Opening   Gregory Nazianzus (c. 329–89)

All things dwell in God alone; to God all things throng in haste.
And God is the end of all things.

Scripture   Revelation 21:1-5 (NRSV)

[1] Then I saw a new heaven and a new earth; for the first heaven and
the first earth had passed away, and the sea was no more.

[2] And I saw the holy city, the new Jerusalem, coming down out of heaven from God, prepared as a bride adorned for her husband.

[3] And I heard a loud voice from the throne saying,

> "See, the home of God is among mortals.
> He will dwell with them;
> they will be his peoples,
> and God himself will be with them;

[4] he will wipe every tear from their eyes.
> Death will be no more;
> mourning and crying and pain will be no more,
> for the first things have passed away."

[5] And the one who was seated on the throne said, "See, I am making all things new." Also he said, "Write this, for these words are trustworthy and true."

A pause for meditation & prayer upon the scripture . . .

Another Voice   Sophie Churchill

> We believe in one God,
> who gave birth to the cosmos and to us,
> creating, out of nothing but his will,
> a world of rocks, plants, and human longing;
> whose eyes will not fail
> to cry for it all.
>
> We believe in one God,
> who redeems the waste of all things good,
> weaving, from the griefs of our freedom,
> new and unhoped-for things;
> whose mercy will not fail
> to heal it all.
>
> We believe in one God,
> who lives among all people in all places,
> calling us from our despair and sleep
> to live out Easter in our generation;
> whose love will not fail
> to hold us all.

Prayer   Henry Vaughan (1621?–95)

> O knowing, glorious Spirit! when
> Thou shalt restore trees, beasts and men,
> When thou shalt make all new again,
> Destroying only death and pain,
> Give him amongst thy works a place,
> Who in them lov'd and sought thy face!

Blessing   The Church of Scotland; *adapted*

> Go in the peace of God,
> in whom there is no darkness,
> but the night shines as the day.
> May God renew your heart with quietness,
> your body with untroubled sleep;
> and may God waken you to use the gift of life
> with faith and joy.

Sunday

Sabbath: The Praise of Creation

MORNING

Opening   *based on* Isaiah 42:10-11

Sing God a new song!
The sea with its creatures,
the coastland and its people,
the desert and the mountains:
let them sing God's praise!

Hymn   *from* "Acclaim with Jubilation"   Brian Wren, 1990

Acclaim with jubilation
   and sing in harmony
with nature's old, evolving,
   unfolding symphony;
the blazing of a comet,
the greening of a planet,
      are songs without a voice
      that bid us all rejoice.

The shrieking of the storm-wind,
   the surging of the seas,
the awestruck alleluias
   that whisper through the trees,
the rushing, booming surf-beat,
the thumping, pulsing heart-beat,
   resound through blood and bone
   to praise the Holy One.
. . . .

Acclaim with jubilation
   the Singer and the Song.
Come out of isolation:
   to sing is to belong.
To God, whose mighty singing

sets all creation ringing,
   lift heart and soul and voice,
   be thankful and rejoice!

Acclaim with Jubilation
Words: Brian Wren

Scripture Psalm 96 from *The Saint Helena Psalter*

[1]   Sing to God a new song;
     sing to God all the whole earth.

[2]   Sing and bless God's holy Name;
     proclaim the good news of salvation from day to day.

[3]   Declare God's glory among the nations,
     God's wonders among all peoples.

[4]   For God is great and greatly to be praised,
     more to be feared than all gods.

[5]   As for all the gods of the nations, they are but idols,
     but it is God who made the heavens.

[6]   Oh, the majesty and magnificence of God's presence!
     Oh, the power and the splendor of God's sanctuary!

[7]   Ascribe to God, you families of the peoples,
     ascribe to God honor and power.

[8]   Ascribe due honor to God's holy Name;
     bring offerings and come into God's courts.

[9]   Worship the Most High in the beauty of holiness;
     let the whole earth tremble before God.

[10] Tell it out among the nations that God reigns!
     God has made the world so firm that it cannot be moved,
     and will judge the peoples with equity.

[11] Let the heavens rejoice, and let the earth be glad;
     let the sea thunder and all that is in it;
       let the field be joyful and all that is therein.

[12] Then shall all the trees of the wood shout for joy
before God, who will come,
     who will come to judge the earth.

[13] God will judge the world with righteousness
and the peoples with truth.

A pause for meditation & prayer upon the scripture . . .

Another Voice   Helder Camara (1909–1999)

The psalms teach us to lend our voice to all creatures: to the mountains and the waters; to the trees and the birds; to the light that comes from above and to the earth that provides for us; to the creatures of the sea, from the tiniest fish to the whale. . . .

Ah, but would you like to have seen the splendor of the act of creation? Then just think, creation is made anew, instant by instant, at God's hands.

Prayer   Thomas Ken (1709), *adapted*

Praise God,
from whom all blessings flow;
praise God, all creatures here below;
praise God above, all heavenly host;
Creator, Christ, and Holy Ghost.
Amen.

Blessing

May you hear today
the song of God's grace unfolding,
the music of the world becoming,
the beating of Christ's own heart
in, with, and under all creation.

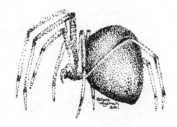

MIDDAY

Reflection   "The Summer Day"   Mary Oliver

Who made the world?
Who made the swan, and the black bear?
Who made the grasshopper?
This grasshopper, I mean—
the one who has flung herself out of the grass,
the one who is eating sugar out of my hand,
who is moving her jaws back and forth instead of up and down—
who is gazing around with her enormous and complicated eyes.
Now she lifts her pale forearms and thoroughly washes her face.
Now she snaps her wings open, and floats away.
I don't know exactly what a prayer is.
I do know how to pay attention, how to fall down
into the grass, how to kneel down in the grass,
how to be idle and blessed, how to stroll through the fields,
which is what I have been doing all day.
Tell me, what else should I have done?
Doesn't everything die at last, and too soon?
Tell me, what is it you plan to do
with your one wild and precious life?

Prayer

You rested this day
from all your making,
and blessed your creation.
   I want to be idle too,
   just like you,
   in your image.
   And I want to be blessed—
   holding some small miracle
   in the palm of my hand today,
   the knees of my pants
   stained by the grass.
      Teach me how
      to pay attention.

EVENING

Opening   *based on* Daniel 3:57

All creation, bless our God,
exalted and glorified forever!

Scripture   Psalm 150 (BARNETT)

[1]   Praise! Praise God in the sanctuary
         and in the highest heavens!
[2]   Praise the Holy One's powerful acts
         and many great deeds.

[3]   Praise God with the sound of the horn,
         with lute and harp.
[4]   Praise the Holy One with timbrels and dancing,
         with strings and pipes.
[5]   Praise God in the clash of cymbals,
         with resounding cymbals.
[6]   Everything that has breath,
         praise, O praise the Holy One!
         Praise the Holy One, Hallelujah!

A pause for meditation & prayer upon the scripture . . .

Another Voice   Leonardo Boff

Above all, we should see the creation as the expression of God's joy, as
the dance of God's love, as the mirror of both God and all created things.
In this sense every creature is a messenger of God, and God's represen-
tative as well as sacrament. Everyone is worthy and is to be accepted
and listened to as such.

Prayer   "Psalm of Gathering"   Daniel J. McGill
         Antiphon: *Shepherd of Love, gather together.*

Gather together, O God of the Universes,
    O God of the Eternities, O God of the Infinities;
Gather together, O God of all names and Gods,
        God of all shadows and lights,
        God of all mysteries;
Gather together, O God, all things
        to worship you and sing your praise.

Gather together, all light and all darkness
Let them behold the wonder of God and worship;
Gather together, all energy and all matter
Let them behold the wonder of God and worship.

Gather together the planets and the stars,
        the galaxies and the quasars,
        the nebulas and the supernovas,
        the black holes and all of the mysteries,

Gather together the particles and the subparticles,
        the atoms and the molecules,
        the forces and the orders,
Let them behold the wonder of God and worship.

Gather together the fossils and the lost,
        the dead and the unknown,
Let them behold the wonder of God and worship.
Gather together the futures and the uncreated,
        the promises and the perils,
        the chaos and the creation,
        the explosion and the gravity,
Let them behold the wonder of God and worship.

Gather together the stones and the elements,
        the liquids and the vapors,
        the clouds and the skies,
        the currents and the convections,
Let them behold the wonder of God and worship.

Gather together the comets and the continents,
        the oceans and the rivers,
        the volcanoes and the sediments,

Let them behold the wonder of God and worship.
Gather together the microbes and the bacteria,
Let them behold the wonder of God and worship.

Gather together the plants and the animals,
    the insects and the ecosystems,
    the intelligent and the instinctive,
Let them behold the wonder of God and worship.

Gather together the spirits of the east and the south,
    the spirits of the west and the north,
    the beings of myth and the creatures of visions,
Let them behold the wonder of God and worship.

Gather together the angels and the archangels,
    the gods and goddesses,
    the demons and the dragons,
Let them behold the wonder of God and worship.

Gather together, O God, and let all be filled
    with reverence,
  for great is your creation, O God;
  beyond all knowing you have made it terrible
    and filled with awe,
  dread and full of wonder.
May joy be the consummation and bliss the communion!

Gather together, O God, gather together!

Blessing   *based on* 2 Thessalonians 3:16

        May the Lord, who is our peace,
       give us peace at all times and in every way.

BIBLE COMMENTS

This section provides a brief historical-theological context for the scriptures used for meditation and prayer each morning and evening. Readers who desire more information may consult other resources such as *The New Oxford Annotated Bible* (New York: Oxford University Press, 1991) or the *Harper's Bible Commentary*, ed. James L. Mays (San Francisco: Harper & Row, 1988). Unless otherwise noted, all scripture citations are from the New Revised Standard Version.

Week One

Monday 1

Genesis 1:1-5

The book of Genesis, a collection of various types of literature from many sources, has four major sections: the initial creation of life and human community (chaps. 1–11), stories centering on Abraham (chaps. 12–25), Jacob (chaps. 25–36), and Joseph (chaps. 37–50). Throughout Genesis, the divine purpose for the people of God directly connects with God's purposes for creation as a whole (e.g., 12:2).

Genesis 1:1-5 are the opening words, not only of this book but of the scriptures that we call the Old and New Testaments. Genesis immediately portrays God as the creator of "the heavens and the earth." In this passage, God creates through the power of divine speech—commanding, inviting, calling the formless or chaotic to order, naming. For God, word and deed are one. Psalm 33:9 will later declare: "For [God] spoke, and it came to be; he commanded, and it stood firm."

This rhythm of divine speech-creation continues beyond this particular passage until the climax at 2:1-3 when God rests and delights in what God has made (see Sunday Morning Prayer, Week One). God also pauses along the way on other days, however, to savor the fact that creation is "good" and even "very good."

John 1:1-5

These majestic opening lines of the Gospel of John echo the opening lines of Genesis (above), taking us back to the "beginning" of creation, and even before the beginning. Christ (the Word) is "with" God, and he "is" God; he is actively involved in bringing all things to life. The light and the life that God speaks into existence in Genesis are now identified in a different way with Christ the Word.

The portrayal of Jesus in the Gospel of John is often loftier than in the other three Gospels: Jesus' language tends to be more poetic and elevated, and his miracles tend more toward the spectacular. Most scholars place the composition of this Gospel at a later time than Matthew, Mark, and Luke, believing that the community that gave us the Letters of John and the book of Revelation also produced this Gospel.

The author (or authors) wants the hearer of this Gospel to understand that the context of Jesus' life, ministry, death, and resurrection is not simply Judea or Galilee or the Roman Empire. From the "beginning" the presence of the Word impacts the whole of creation.

Tuesday 1

Psalm 145:8-9, 13*b*-16

The book of Psalms is actually several books or collections (perhaps five) woven together over time, brought together most definitively during a period when the people and institutions of Israel were emerging from military defeat and exile in Babylon (587–538 BCE). While scholars disagree as to particulars, some of the psalms may be as ancient as the time of David's kingship (c. 1000 BCE), while most may have been composed just before or during the time of exile.

The book of Psalms has long been regarded as the original and supreme "prayer book" of the people of God—expressing to God deep emotions, from despair and anger to hope and joy. John Calvin once described the Psalms as "an anatomy of all parts of the soul"; but the psalms always speak of a human soul living in relation to others: God, neighbor, nation, friend, enemy, and the larger creation.

Psalm 145 is a prayer of praise or adoration. These particular lines give evidence of why God is so worthy of praise: God is continually gracious, merciful, faithful, and generous, providing for the needs of every creature.

John 1:14, 16, 18

These verses bring to a climax the testimony begun in John 1:1 (see Monday Evening Prayer). The Word who was in the "beginning" with God, is God, and through whom everything that exists has come to life—this same Word "became flesh and lived among us." These words point to Christ, of course, and to the mystery of what we have come to call the Incarnation.

This stunning affirmation states that the Creator not only shapes and watches over the creation but actually becomes part of it—a member of the human species—in Jesus of Nazareth. God chooses to care for creation and redeem it by becoming fully embodied within it.

Wednesday 1

Psalm 19:1-6

This psalm in its entirety celebrates the glory of God, both as Creator (vv. 1-6) and as the source of life-enhancing law (vv. 7-13). Many scholars believe that the first half was crafted during the time of David (c. 1000 BCE) and the second half from the post-exilic time of Ezra (c. 428 BCE). These two halves combine, however, to ground both "creation" and "law" as products of a gracious and ingenious God.

These verses (vv. 1-6) highlight the way in which everyday, natural phenomena reveal—with a nonverbal eloquence—something of the luminous glory that is God. The poetry lingers especially upon the daily arc of the sun, comparing the sun's course and energy to that of a bridegroom emerging from his lover's tent or an athlete running a race.

Sirach 42:16; 43:1-5

Sirach is attributed to a man of wisdom named Ben Sira (or Son of Sirach), who was active around 200 to 180 BCE. Sirach bridges the wisdom traditions of the older Jewish scriptures (such as the book of Proverbs) with the philosophical influences of the ascending Greek or Hellenic culture.

The verses for this evening are an excerpt from a psalm or "hymn" offered in praise of the Creator, which focuses on the ways the sun reveals (or "proclaims," 43:2) the marvelous wisdom and inventiveness of God.

Thursday 1

Genesis 1:24-31

This morning's reading returns to the first chapter of Genesis (see Monday Morning Prayer) and its story of creation. On the "sixth day," God creates everything that lives upon the earth's surface, including humankind, and then declares it all "very good."

This text has inspired much debate throughout the centuries, for the most part centered on what it may mean for humankind to be created in the "image "of God (v. 27) and to receive "dominion" (v. 28) over "every living thing." For Christians who take seriously both the Bible and our present-day ecological crisis, these urgent questions demand thoughtful prayer and prayerful thought.

Genesis 2:4-8, 15

The translation by Mary Phil Korsak from *At the Start: Genesis Made New* has the merit of bringing into English some of the "earthy" qualities, connotations, and punning of the original Hebrew. Korsak translates the Hebrew words *'adam* and *'adamah* as "groundling" and "ground," thus graphically linking our "human" origins with the "humus." We are earthlings formed from the earth and enlivened by God's breath.

These verses come from the so-called "second creation account," crafted by a different tradition from Genesis 1, which uses a different name for God (translated in the NRSV as the "LORD God"). This passage does not mention the "image of God" or "dominion." Here humankind's purpose is to "serve" and "keep" the garden.

Friday 1

Jeremiah 12:10-13

The book bearing the name of Jeremiah is actually several different collections edited together into its present form. This complex, nonchronological compilation alternates between prophetic oracles, laments, memoirs, poetry, and prose. Many of the oracles may have their origin in the historical Jeremiah (c. 626–587 BCE), who lived in Judah during the final decades before its siege and defeat by Babylon.

Walter Brueggemann gives one of the best, single-sentence descriptions of the prophets of the Old Testament (indeed, of any prophetic figure): "They see what others do not see, and they dare to utter what others would not dare to utter."[1] What others could not or would not see and name, Jeremiah did. He believed the kingdom of Judah had forsaken its covenant with God, as evidenced by its systemic, political, and religious corruption and social disparities. In Jeremiah's vision, the armies of Babylon and Egypt were enacting God's just response to Judah's corruption. But even in the midst of Judah's downfall, Jeremiah also saw reason for hope: the days were coming when God would yet restore God's people (30:3).

The selected verses for this morning (12:10-13) are spoken by God, grieving the desolation of the land and its people due to the corruption, greed, and mismanagement of Judah's political/religious leadership, the elite ("shepherds").

The present desolation will be made worse by the coming warfare, which will further spoil and devour the land. If anger is "love with a wound," as someone once said, then the Creator speaks here as one who has been mightily wounded by the people God loves.

Psalm 107:33-43

This particular psalm opens the fifth "book" or collection within the Psalms. The psalm gives thanks for God's deliverance from many difficult situations: wandering through desert wastelands (vv. 4-9), imprisonment (vv. 10-16), sin and disease (vv. 17-22), and being tossed about at sea (vv. 23-32). Many scholars believe that verses 33-43 were added to the psalm after the period of exile in Babylon because they refer to an experience of seeing a land laid waste and then brought back to life by God.

These verses also contain an explicit warning: what God has caused or allowed to happen once ("rivers into a desert," "fruitful land into a salty waste"), God may cause or allow to happen again. God's blessing of flowing water, fertile valleys, rich harvests, food for all will hinge upon the righteousness of the people and their leaders—a righteousness which, like God's, looks to the needs of the poor in the land.

Saturday 1

Psalm 145

So revered is this psalm within Judaism, it is daily recited in synagogue at morning, noonday, and evening prayer. The psalm repeatedly calls us to join in praising God, moved and motivated by the great works God has done and is doing.

Among God's great and ongoing works is the giving of food to "every living thing" and responding to all those who "call sincerely." The psalm perceives these as acts of divine salvation and calls upon "all flesh" (human and other-than-human) to join in blessing God's name.

John 3:16-17

The reformer Martin Luther (1438–1546) once called John 3:16 the "gospel in miniature." It is worth noting that several words in this passage could be variously translated. The word translated in both verses as "world" is, in the Greek original, "cosmos." The word *saved* in verse 17 may also be translated as "healed" or "made whole" (as it is in other places). And the word *everyone* in verse 16 is *pas* in the Greek, signifying all things. (This word, is also used in John 12:32: "And I, when I am lifted up from the earth, will draw *all things* to myself"; and in Colossians 1:17: "He himself is before *all things*, and in him *all things* hold together.")

Taking the meaning and connotations of these words into account, according to the Gospel of John the "good news" of God's gift to us of the only Son is not about the "personal" salvation of individual human souls (only) from this world to some other—but rather the healing and recreation of the entire cosmos (humans included).

Sunday 1

Genesis 2:1-3

These are the climactic verses of the first creation account (Gen. 1:1–2:3). The seventh day (sabbath) is "blessed" and "hallowed" by God, because on this day God rested.

Many scholars believe that this text was created, compiled, and/or edited during the postexilic period (from c. 500–450 BCE) by people of God who shared a priestly perspective or concern for the reemerging nation. Other texts from this source tend to deal with matters of proper ritual, sacrifice, and so on. This particular text underscores the importance of "keeping sabbath" in the weekly calendar because *God* is the one who established sabbath as part of the original rhythm of creation.

Psalm 131

The first week's cycle of prayer concludes with this lovely psalm that offers a maternal image of God. Psalm 131 both describes and evokes an atmosphere of humility, rest, and trust.

Week Two

Monday 2

Isaiah 40:12-25

Isaiah 40–55 is often referred to as *Second* Isaiah because the author (or authors) of these chapters seems to be different from the prophet Isaiah who lived during the last days of the reign of King Uzziah (c. 742 BCE). These chapters are referred to as Second *Isaiah* because (1) they are included as part of the book or scroll of Isaiah, and (2) they seem to have originated within a community of persons preserving and carrying forward the oracles and teachings of the original Isaiah.

The content of chapters 40–55 presupposes that the people of Judah are in captivity or exile in Babylon (c. 586–539 BCE), perhaps near the end of this period (c. 550–540). While First Isaiah declares the coming collapse of Jerusalem/Judah (e.g., 6:9ff.), Second Isaiah proclaims that God will soon liberate the people of Judah from their imprisonment. Such words are spoken strongly in chapter 40, the first chapter of Second Isaiah.

In the verses for today's reading, the intent is to calm whatever fears the captive people of God may have about the power of nations such as Babylon. These verses affirm that God *alone* is the Creator of everything and that justice and understanding ultimately reside in the hands of this same God. The speaker asks a series of questions—Who? Who? Whom? Who?—a rhetorical device underscoring the unique power and wisdom of God the Creator.

Romans 11:33-36

Of all the books of the New Testament, aside from the four Gospels, the book of Romans has had the greatest influence on the shape of Christian theology. Counted among the letters of Paul, Romans was likely composed sometime between 54 and 58 CE. He may have intended it for a particular audience (1:7: "To all God's beloved in Rome"), but the letter seems to have been quickly and widely shared throughout the Mediterranean region.

Paul proclaims that the gospel of Christ is God's power and means for bringing about the salvation or redemption of all who place their trust in this God—indeed, the means through which God is redeeming all creation (see 8:19ff.). Our verses for today are a celebratory conclusion to a longer section (chapters 9–11) in which Paul discerns the mysterious movement of God's grace—from the ancient promises to Abraham and Moses to the inclusion ("grafting," see 11:17ff.) of Gentiles.

Verse 34 may sound familiar because Paul is quoting Isaiah 40:13 (above) and to the same effect: God *alone*, the wise Creator of all things, could do such a thing as this! "For from him and through him and to him are all things" (11:36). This is, for Paul, all the more reason to praise and glorify God.

Tuesday 2

Psalm 104:1-2*a*, 10-24

This psalm is a hymn of praise to God the Creator. In many ways, the first half of the psalm is a further poetic rendering of the first creation account, in that the psalm echoes many elements of God's creating in Genesis 1:1-2:4*a*: light (vv. 1-2*a*); sky or firmament (vv. 2*b*-4); earth and heaven (vv. 5-9); moon and sun (vv. 19-20); ocean creatures (vv. 25-26); earthbound creatures, including humankind (vv. 21-23); and a pause for delight (v. 24).

Psalm 104 not only celebrates God as Maker; it also affirms God's *ongoing* care and provision for all that God has made. God makes "springs gush forth in the valleys," providing water for thirsty beasts, trees, and birds. God makes "grass to grow for the cattle," "plants for people," and so forth. All life flows from God, sustained by God's active involvement within creation.

Genesis 8:20-22

These verses come from the story of Noah, the ark, and the Flood (Gen. 6:5–8:22). At this point in the story, the flood waters have receded; the ark rests on dry ground; and Noah has now stepped out of the ark for the first time, together with his family and all the creatures. Noah's first act on dry land involves engaging in ritual worship of the Lord (presumably sacrificing some of the very animals he had preserved onboard).

Despite the inevitability of human sin, God promises never again to "destroy every living creature." God vows to remain faithful and merciful; the regularity of seasons and sunlight underscores this promise. God reaffirms these promises in Genesis 9:1-17 and makes it even more explicit that this covenant is with "every living creature," not simply the human species.

Wednesday 2

Proverbs 30:18-19, 24-28

The book of Proverbs is a collection of "wisdom" teachings. While often attributed to Solomon (who had a reputation for great wisdom), Proverbs contains at least seven collections from various times. Its final form came sometime after the period of exile, perhaps even as late as c. 300 BCE.

The wisdom traditions in the Bible assume that in order to live a successful or happy life a person needs to pay attention to the world around him or her. God has woven many life-giving rules and rhythms into the very fabric of creation. Pay attention and learn.

Today's passages pay attention to many things: an eagle, a snake, a ship, a man and a woman, ants, badgers, locusts, lizards. What may we see and learn from even the smallest creatures that we may apply to our own lives?

Ecclesiastes 3:1-11

Like the book of Proverbs, Ecclesiastes is a collection of wisdom teachings, probably finalized as we know it c. 300 BCE. Scholars do not agree about the book's authorship or thematic organization—or if Ecclesiastes means to *confirm* the conventional wisdom of Hebraic culture (as represented, for example, in the book of Proverbs) or *undermine* it (e.g., 1:2: "All is vanity").

R. B. Y. Scott writes that Ecclesiastes fulfills a needed role within the Bible: that of "warning against human hubris and preserving divine mystery."[2]

Today's passage is a poem (3:1-8) that affirms there is a fit and proper time "for every matter under heaven." The prose verses immediately following the poem (3:9ff.) state that humans can understand a limited amount about God's purposes. Does our human finitude in the face of eternity invite resignation or lead us to place of awe in God's presence? Ecclesiastes seems to want to validate both responses while "preserving divine mystery."

Thursday 2

Psalm 8

This psalm of praise affirms in both the opening and closing verses that the glory of God's name resounds "through all the earth" (NAB). The psalm never completely answers the question that it asks: What is humankind that God should care for it? The human race is dwarfed by the vastness of the heavens; yet God invests humankind with dignity by giving it "dominion" over God's creation. The psalm returns us theologically to Genesis 1:26-31 and to the questions raised earlier about the meaning of "dominion" and "image of God." Walter Brueggemann deals with the issues this way:

> With the gift of dominion intrinsic to human personhood comes immense responsibility, for the work of humankind is to care for the earth even as the Creator has already begun to care, to protect and enhance the earth as God's creation.[3]

Who are we then? Measured on the scales of deep time and cosmic space, we shrink to insignificance. Yet God entrusts us with responsibility to "protect and enhance" the creation.

Philippians 4:4-9

Although scholars disagree about where and when this letter was written (many argue for Rome c. 61–63 CE, while others propose Ephesus in the mid-50s), they do not disagree that this is a letter from the apostle Paul to the Christian community in Philippi. Paul thanks that community for the gifts it has sent him in his imprisonment (4:18) and encourages the Philippians to join him in remaining steadfast and joyful in the faith.

Paul states why he and the Philippians may rejoice in the Lord: "the Lord is near" (v. 5*b*). Not only is the time of Christ's return approaching, but he is even now among them. Therefore they may rejoice and pray with surety that God is guarding their lives in Christ Jesus.

Paul then encourages the Philippians to attend to the presence of God that is manifested by the excellencies that surround them in creation and culture: whatever is true, honorable, just, pure, pleasing, commendable, etc. In so doing they may find strength and peace to continue in the way of discipleship.

Friday 2

Jeremiah 4:22-26

[For more information on Jeremiah, see comments on Friday 1.] Terence Fretheim calls this text "one of the most vivid biblical portrayals of environmental catastrophe."[4] The vision of the prophet in verses 23-26 is of a creation undone: everything is ruined and lifeless.

For Jeremiah, this environmental destruction is a visitation of God's anger upon the land, people, and creatures of Judah—a result, directly or indirectly, of the people's foolishness and evil. Human behavior (for good or ill), the health of creation, and God's mercy and justice are interrelated in one divine, ecological whole.

Isaiah 33:7-10

Although this chapter falls within the section (chaps. 1–39) often referred to as First Isaiah, its source is not the prophet himself. According to scholars, it is probably a later, postexilic addition to the scroll. Chapter 33 appears to be a composite of prayers recognizing (after the fact) the validity of Isaiah's earlier prophecies and praying for God's deliverance.

The selection of verses for this evening expresses the same worldview as Jeremiah 4 (above): a breakdown of justice within the community of God's people (vv. 7-8) reflects a breakdown within the larger natural order (v. 9). The selection ends at verse 10 with the Lord's arising to take action.

Saturday 2

2 Corinthians 5:17-18

When we peruse Paul's letters it is important to remember that we are reading someone else's mail. We have in hand only one side of a conversation—Paul's, which may leave us confused as to the problems or issues he is addressing. This seems especially true with Second Corinthians, a letter that many scholars believe may actually be more than one letter stitched together by a later editor.

Our verses for this morning come from a section of Second Corinthians in which Paul defends his calling and authority as an apostle of Christ. Paul believes his critics are regarding him as Paul once regarded Christ: "from a human point of view." But Paul's point of view was forever transformed (as should be that of his critics) by his experience of the risen Christ.

"If anyone is in Christ, there is a new creation," Paul writes (v. 17). The creation is made "new" because the one who is in Christ now shares in God's work of reconciling heaven and earth. God's purpose in Christ is to shape a "new creation" in which the relationship among God, humankind, and the whole creation is renewed.

Hosea 2:18-20

The prophet Hosea spoke to the people of the Northern Kingdom (sometimes called Israel or even Samaria) in the last decades before its defeat by the Assyrian army (c. 722/721). In his view, the people had become unfaithful to the Lord, forsaking true faith for the worship of Baal. Hosea used his own marriage to an unfaithful wife, Gomer, to illustrate the message that Israel was likewise being unfaithful to God and playing "the whore" with Baal.

But the book of Hosea also contains messages of hope and reconciliation. In today's passage the voice of God speaks, using the metaphor of marriage (vv. 19-20), to say that God will again take Israel as God's "wife forever." On God's initiative the marriage will be renewed "in righteousness and in justice, in steadfast love, and in mercy" (v. 19b). God makes this covenant not only with the people but with the "wild animals, the birds of the air, and the creeping things of the ground" (v. 18). The land will become a place of peace and safety, not war.

In other readings from the prophets (Second Isaiah, Jeremiah) we have seen how human sinfulness negatively impacts the health of the earth. In this passage we see that the opposite is also the case: God's love, mercy, and forgiveness can restore or recreate all life, human and nonhuman.

Sunday 2

Psalm 148

This hymn of praise calls on all creation—heaven and earth—to join in singing. But *how* is this to be accomplished? How does the sun or the moon, the fruit trees or the cedars, praise God?

According to Terence Fretheim, the psalm states that all parts of creation should praise God simply due to the *fact* of their creation by God. God has created sun, moon, stars, sea creatures, fire, snow, and all types of people and given them a place within the created order. "Praise occurs when the creature fulfills the task for which it was created."[5]

Song of Solomon 2:8-13

Roland Murphy has written that what distinguishes the Song of Songs most sharply from the rest of the Old Testament is the "exuberant, thoroughly erotic, and nonjudgmental manner in which it depicts the love between a man and a woman."[6] Although this collection of love lyrics celebrates human sexual desire and fulfillment, many readers have also interpreted the Song of Solomon as an allegory for the love between God and Israel, the church, or the human soul.

In tonight's passage, the woman's lover calls her to "arise" and "come away" with him. Just as the earth is bursting and blooming with beauty, so is his desire for her. Gazelles, stags, flowers, turtledoves, fig trees, men, women: each in its own way is driven or drawn into a dance of sexuality that is part of the mystery and delight of God's creation.

Week Three

Monday 3

Genesis 1:14-19

[For more on Genesis and the first creation account, see Monday 1.]
We begin Week Three by returning once more to the first creation account. In these verses God creates what we refer to as the sun and the moon ("the two great lights," v. 16) and the stars. According to Genesis, God creates these lights in order to separate or distinguish day from night and one season or year from another. In a sense, the sun, moon, and stars not only "give light upon the earth" but also allow the creatures of earth to measure the passage of time.

Some scholars hear in these lines a subversive, "antimonarchial" note. In the context of Babylonian rule, where the people of Israel had been held in exile, "the word of the monarch was law, absolutely, and that word dominated both people and nature at will."[7] But here in Genesis, the sun and the moon are subject only to God their Creator—not to any human king, Babylonian or otherwise. Furthermore, the Creator then entrusts to the sun and moon the power to "rule" the day and the night on God's behalf (v. 16). God gives the creation its own inherent order and integrity. And again, God sees it all to be "good."

2 Corinthians 4:5-6

Paul defends the authenticity of his ministry over against those (unnamed) who are questioning his authority. Rather than promoting himself, Paul claims that he has in every way directed the people's attention to Christ. The gospel he proclaims in word and deed has been completely transparent, with nothing veiled and no hidden agendas. Everything is out in the open and in the light—God's light.

Light as metaphor connects Paul to Christ, Christ to God the Father-Creator, and Paul's ministry to God's purposes. Paul affirms that the glory of the same God who said, "Let there be light" (Gen. 1:3), shines in "the face of Jesus Christ"; this light now also shines in Paul's own heart (or "our hearts," v. 6). But light is also more than metaphor for Paul: in the book of Acts (9:1ff.; 22:6ff.) it is a blinding light from heaven and the voice of Christ that redirects the course of Paul's life and faith.

Tuesday 3

Matthew 6:25-33

The Gospel of Matthew was probably composed around 90 CE in or near the city of Antioch in Syria. The author may have been a Jewish Christian and, like his audience or congregation, a second-generation follower of Christ. Matthew contains much of the same material as the Gospels of Mark and Luke (it is believed that Matthew and Luke share Mark as a common source); but more than Mark and Luke, the Gospel of Matthew seems to emphasize Jesus the Messiah ("Christ") as the true founder of a "new Israel," one who lives and teaches a new and "higher" righteousness.

Jesus the Teacher speaks at length in Matthew, especially in five separate speeches or "discourses" (chaps. 5–7; 10; 13; 18; 24–25). Our passage for this morning is an excerpt from his first discourse, the Sermon on the Mount, spoken by Jesus to his disciples and, indirectly, to the crowd gathered on the hillside. As Moses once did long ago, Jesus (the new Moses) now delivers God's truth to the people.

In 6:25-33 Jesus addresses the causes of anxiety among the people: basic human needs such as food, drink, and clothing. But Jesus directs the hearers' attention to the nonhuman creation and to the way in which his Father provides for the birds, the lilies, and the grass. God's providential care for the larger creation should inspire us to trust in God's care for humanity. "First things first," Jesus seems to be saying. "Strive first for the kingdom of God and his righteousness," and everything else will fall into place.

Note that the "higher righteousness" of Jesus includes, for his disciples, a mandate of generous care for the poor, the hungry, the sick, and the imprisoned (Matt. 25:31-46).

Psalm 23

This psalm expresses trust in God's guidance and protection. According to Carroll Stuhlmueller, the early church sang this psalm as newly baptized people emerged from the font to then walk toward the "prepared table" of the Eucharist.[8] Today the psalm is a welcome scripture at funerals, reminding believers that God walks with us even through the "valley of the shadow of death" (KJV).

Whenever or however the psalm is used, it nearly always accomplishes its purpose: it inspires us with confidence in God's care (v. 1: "there is nothing I lack"), especially in the face of adversity (v. 4: "I fear no harm"), and moves us to give thanks both for what we have received from God's hand (v. 2: rest, food, water; v. 3: strength, guidance, security,; v. 4: comfort and courage in adversity; v. 5: table and drink, soothing oil) and what we are promised (v. 6: to "dwell in the house of the LORD for years to come").

Wednesday 3

The Book of Job

Our two selections of scripture for today are from Job. Little is known about the author or authors of Job or the time of its composition and/or editing—except that its language (mostly poetry) is an elegant, learned Hebrew. Although there is no hard evidence, most scholars date the final form of the book in the postexilic period.

Job is classified among the wisdom literature of the Old Testament due to the abundance of wisdom themes that appear within it—but Job also questions the conventional wisdom related to God's justice (i.e., that God rewards the "good" and punishes the "bad"). For as the story or legend is told, the heavenly "Prosecutor" (sometimes translated "the satan") pressures God into allowing the Prosecutor to test the steadfastness of Job, a man known for his honesty and uprightness. In quick order Job suffers the loss of his wealth, children, and health—and, although Job refuses to curse God for his suffering, he does demand an explanation.

Three friends appear (Eliphaz, Bildad, and Zophar), first to comfort Job and then in various ways to answer his demands for an explanation by defending God's justice. The three are later joined by a fourth person, Elihu. Their responses reflect the themes of conventional wisdom and satisfy neither Job nor the reader (for the reader knows, with Job, that he is "innocent" of wrongdoing); so Job calls on God for an answer.

At last God appears "out of the whirlwind" (38:1) and, rather than answering Job directly, begins to ask *Job* a long series of hard questions.

What is the end result of the dialogue between God and Job? It is hard to say. We learn that Job's so-called friends are wrong; the traditional wisdom concerning God's justice does not apply to Job's situation (and if it does not to his, then perhaps not to other situations of success or suffering). We learn that, while neither Job in particular nor humankind in general are necessarily the focal points of God's creation, God does care for those who are faithful.

The book closes with Job and God reconciled (somewhat): Job's wealth is doubled; he has more children and dies "old and full of days" (42:17). And yet, for most readers, many questions remain.

Job 12:7-10

These verses fall within Job's extended reply (chaps. 12–14) to the first discourses of his three friends, whose explanations have offered him neither comfort nor clarity in his suffering. Their wisdom is insufficient, their "maxims are proverbs of ashes" (13:12). Even the beasts, the birds, the plants, and the fish have greater wisdom than these three men. "Talk to the animals," Job tells the three, and they will testify to true workings of God's power.

Although Job may speak these words to his friends in anger or sarcasm, he expresses a presumption within biblical wisdom—that there is an inherent knowledge of God within the created order, the nonhuman as well as the human; and that humankind may have something to learn from "listening" to the rest of God's creation.

Job 38:1-7

God's response to Job (chaps. 38–41) begins with a brief interruption by Job in 40:3-5. Rather than answering Job and addressing the question of human suffering, God speaks a series of questions that leaves Job nearly speechless.

In verses 4-7 God directs Job's attention to the beginnings of creation. Where were you (Job) when I (God) laid the earth's foundation? Where were you when the morning stars first sang? From here God's speech continues, directing Job's attention to different aspects of God's creation—some wonderful, some terrifying; but all part of God's mysterious workings.

God's speech implies that God is and will always remain at the center of creation, not Job and not humankind—and that while God's ways may be knowable to some degree, God is ultimately beyond our human wisdom or control. God cannot be "tamed" by any human categories.

Thursday 3

Wisdom of Solomon 9:1-3, 4*a*

Like Sirach, the Wisdom of Solomon is part of the Apocrypha—books included in the ancient Greek and Latin translations of scripture but not ordinarily used by Jewish or Protestant adherents. Although the author of Wisdom assumes the authority of Solomon (9:7-8, 12), the book was most likely composed during the first century BCE by an unknown Jewish author, writing in Greek, for a community of Jews living in Alexandria. According to Roland Murphy, the book "stands out as intensely Jewish and, at the same time, thoroughly stamped by Greek culture."[9]

Today's three verses are part of a longer prayer for wisdom (8:17–9:18) who is spoken of and addressed as a woman ("Sophia" or "Lady Wisdom"). Lady Wisdom embodies the Creator's providential care for creation and is an expression of God's glory, power, light, and goodness. Verses 1-3 affirm that God created all things in wisdom and that humankind's purpose or vocation is to care for God's creatures with holiness, justice, and "uprightness of soul." To accomplish this, humankind needs the guidance and companionship of Lady Wisdom.

Micah 6:6-8

The prophet Micah lived in the countryside southwest of Jerusalem in the Southern Kingdom of Judah, a younger contemporary of the prophet Isaiah (or "first Isaiah"). He was also affected by the fall of the Northern Kingdom of Israel to the Assyrians (722/21 BCE), and the Assyrian threat to Jerusalem and Judah. Like Isaiah, Micah believed that Israel and Judah were being punished for their sin—a sinfulness due, in no small part, to the corruption of the nations' religious-political-economic leaders.

Our scripture for this evening comes from a portion of Micah that portrays God as filing a lawsuit ("controversy," 6:2) against Judah. Creation is summoned to the trial—the mountains, hills, and the "foundations of the earth" will serve as witnesses and jury—with the verdict announced in 6:9ff.

The unidentified speaker of verses 6-8 issues a clear message: God has shown the nations what is "good." They are to do justice, love kindness, and walk humbly with their God. From Micah's perspective, verse 8 expresses the true vocation of God's people. Religious ceremony and ritual are meaningless without a commitment to justice (social-economic-political), relationships guided by kindness, and a humble companionship with God.

Friday 3

Deuteronomy 11:13-17

Most likely, the book of Deuteronomy was originally addressed to the Northern Kingdom of Israel about the eighth century BCE. Its final form, however, dates from the time of Israel's exile in Babylonia, a time when a faint hope flickered among its hearers for a return to their home.

Deuteronomy records three long discourses (1:6–4:40; 5–28; 29–30) of Moses, which reaffirm the covenant traditions of the book of Exodus. The divine commandments and laws of Exodus are not simply repeated verbatim, however: they are reinterpreted to speak to a new generation.

Our verses for today come just before Moses (re)proclaims God's laws in chapters 12–26. He encourages the people to obey the laws they are about to hear, for obedience will mean "life" and "blessing," while disobedience will mean "death" and "curse"—not simply for the people and the nation but for the land itself. The modern consciousness often chafes at this theology, labeled by some as "deuteronomistic"—that God so neatly rewards the obedient and punishes the disobedient. Interestingly, the Bible itself often questions this theology—most notably in the book of Job.

And yet we need not dismiss too quickly Deuteronomy's worldview, which assumes that to obey God's laws is "to live in harmony with God's intentions for the creation."[10] Deuteronomy also assumes, as do the books of the prophets, that an interconnectedness exists between the (human) moral order and the cosmic order, such that human sin—whether religious, political, social, or economic—will have a destructive effect upon the nonhuman environment. Many contemporary social and environmental scientists (regardless of religion) share a similar assumption.

Hosea 4:1-3

[See Saturday 2 for additional background on Hosea.]
The voice of God speaks in these verses, announcing that God has an "indictment" or "controversy" with Israel. (Compare this with Micah 6.) God's list of grievances is long: faithlessness, disloyalty, ignorance of God, swearing, lying, murder, theft, adultery, and "bloodshed follows bloodshed." Notice how the prophet then connects human sinfulness to the devastation of the *non*human creation: "Therefore the land mourns. . . . "

Environmentalists often say that the rich destroy the earth out of greed, while the poor destroy the earth out of need—that wherever and whenever economic imbalances exist (such as between "First World" and "Third World" or between the nations of the Northern and Southern hemispheres), the earth itself also suffers. When the "wild animals" and the "birds of the air" languish, when species become extinct ("the fish of the sea are perishing"), when air is polluted, forests denuded, and soils eroded—this may result from broken *human* relationships and misconduct.

Saturday 3

Isaiah 11:6-9

We have previously reflected on passages from "Second" or "Deutero" Isaiah (Monday and Friday, Week Two)—scripture emerging from later followers of the prophet. Today's scripture is probably original to the actual historical person: Isaiah of Jerusalem, who lived in the Southern Kingdom of Judah from the reign of King Uzziah (c. 742 BCE) until the end of the reign of Hezekiah (c. 687/6 BCE). According to James M. Efird, the prophet appears to have been "a highly educated man, one who served as court counselor to the kings, and he may even have been a member of the priestly circles as well."[11]

Isaiah sees much to condemn in his own nation, the nation of Israel, and the surrounding nations; but his oracles also give reason to hope. Although the reign of King Ahaz (c. 735–716 BCE) was thoroughly faithless and corrupt in the eyes of the prophet, the Lord God would raise up a new king: one upon whom the "spirit of the LORD" would rest. This new king or "messiah" would judge the poor with righteousness (unlike Ahaz) and "decide with equity for the meek of the earth" (11:4).

Today's verses envision the time of Messiah as a rebirth or recreation, not only for the people but for all creation. No more "predators" (wolf, leopard, bear, lion, asp) and "prey" (lamb, kid, calf, child): all creation, human and nonhuman, will live in the fullness of peace.

Colossians 1:15-20

Contemporary scholars disagree whether Paul or one of his followers actually wrote this letter. The letter itself claims Paul as author, but the letter's style and vocabulary suggest someone else.

Colossae, once an important trading center in the region of Asia Minor, was a crossroads of many religious practices. The threat to its nascent Christian community and to which the letter speaks was a form of "syncretism." Elements from other faiths were being blended into the community in a way that undermined the supremacy of Christ. In answer to this, the letter to the Colossians repeatedly affirms the centrality of Christ's life, death, and resurrection to the faith. Bruce Metzger believes that "there is no stronger affirmation of the lordship of Christ in the New Testament."[12]

In 1:15-20, the author quotes the lyrics of a hymn—perhaps one familiar to the Colossian church. The hymn not only claims Christ as "head of the body, the church" (v. 18) but also as the "firstborn of all creation" (v. 15). Indeed, the universe was created "through him and for him" (v. 16) and is held together by Christ (v. 17). Christ is "lord" or "head" not only of the church but of the entire cosmos.

The hymn places the cross of Christ at the center of God's purposes for creation. By the "blood of his cross," Christ reconciles all creation with God's original intent for all life: peace, wholeness, shalom (v. 20).

Sunday 3

Exodus 20:8-11

Like Genesis, the book of Exodus weaves together various strands of tradition. It is, as James M. Efird says, "the product of centuries of having been passed along both orally and in written form."[13] The two grand movements within the book, accounting for the emergence of the Hebrew faith, are the exodus from slavery in Egypt and the transmission of God's laws. The nation of Israel, emerging in the wilderness, now becomes the bearer of the promise made to Abraham and Sarah: that God would bless them and, through them, bless the whole creation.

In Genesis 2:1-3, the Creator rests on the "seventh day" and declares it holy—thereby establishing rest and even the savoring of life as part of the fundamental rhythm of creation. In Exodus 20:8-11, marking off time to rest on the sabbath now receives the force of divine law; indeed, it is part of the Ten Commandments.

Keep in mind the biblical mind-set that views all of life as interconnected—divine, human, nonhuman—and that God's commandments are given in order that *all* life may flourish. When the people of God, including their animals, take time to rest and delight in life (which includes the worship or savoring of God), allowing the earth also to rest, all creation benefits and receives blessing.

Daniel 3:74-83 (NJB)

These verses are an excerpt from a longer canticle, often referred to as the "Song of the Three Youths." The narrative setting is the story from the book of Daniel of the three Jewish young men, ordered by King Nebuchadnezzar to be thrown into the "fiery furnace." The three remain steadfast in their faith, praying and singing praise to God even in the furnace—and emerge unharmed. As is evident from this excerpt, the three youths call upon all creation to join them in praising the God of Israel.

The "Song of the Three Youths" is a later edition to the book of Daniel, itself written during the oppressive reign of Antiochus Epiphanes, 167–164 BCE.

Week Four

· *Monday 4*

Psalm 139:13-18

This psalm is perhaps the most personal, intimate expression of faith within the Old Testament. From start to finish, the psalmist affirms himself as "known" by God—not only today but from the beginning of his life within his mother's womb (v. 13). The same God who created the heavens and the earth also creates each person, "knitting" the body together. The psalmist expresses awe at God's creative genius.

Hebrews 11:1-3

Little is known for certain about the origin and authorship of the letter to the Hebrews. Judging by its literary form, Hebrews is not a letter; its intended readership may or may not have been "Hebrews" (i.e., Jews or Jewish Christians); and Paul was probably not its author. Nevertheless, the book inspires readers to stand firm in the faith, trusting in Christ and in "a great cloud of witnesses" (12:1) who laid the foundations for belief.

Chapter 11 begins by defining faith or trust as "the assurance of things hoped for, the conviction of things not seen" and then gives a roll call (11:4-40) of many of the great heroes who lived this faith (including such luminaries as Noah, Abraham and Sarah, Isaac and Jacob, Joseph, Moses, Samuel, David, and the prophets). These are among the "ancestors" who "received approval" from God because of their faith (v. 2).

But according to Hebrews, our faith leads us to trust God as the Creator who "prepared" the worlds from the beginning, a conviction not based on what any human has "seen."

Tuesday 4

Joel 2:21-24

Although some of the material incorporated in the book of Joel may be older, the book probably came to its final form in or near Judah around the time of the military conquests and death of Alexander the Great (323 BCE). Joel opens with a vision of destruction brought about by a "destroying locust" (1:4ff.). Scholars disagree about whether this reference is literal (an actual plague of insects) or figurative (the effects of a marauding army). "Locust" was a common metaphor in ancient times for invading armies. Nevertheless, the people and land have been devastated.

With 2:18, however, the tone of Joel shifts significantly. In response to the suffering of people and land and in response to the nation's penitential return to the Lord, God promises to restore the soil, the animals, and the plants (vv. 21-22). Joel calls the people to rejoice over God's gift of rain that brings with it the promise of threshing floors "full of grain" and vats overflowing with wine and oil (v. 24). The flourishing of creation, temporarily disrupted by "swarming locust," now continues.

Psalm 65:5-13

According to James L. Mays, these verses of Psalm 65 praise God as the "cosmic farmer."[14] Listen to the actions ascribed to God: tending and watering land, filling springs, readying seed, preparing grain. God waters or softens the land with rain (v. 10), thus blessing the land with growth. The thumb of this Cosmic Farmer is decidedly green. All God touches comes alive, causing the mountains and meadows to "shout and sing together for joy" (v. 13).

Wednesday 4

Jeremiah 17:7-8 (Morning) and Psalm 1:1-3 (Evening)

Many commentators believe that the verses from Jeremiah 17 may be modeled on the ones from Psalm 1 (tonight's reading). Both readings speak of those who are blessed or happy and compare them to well-rooted, healthy trees. In the case of Jeremiah, trusting in God brings such blessings (17:7); in Psalm 1, it is delighting in God's law (1:2). Perhaps to do one is also to do the other.

Both readings often fall under the classification of wisdom teachings, a tradition that commonly compares wisdom to a tree. In Proverbs 3:18 we also read that "she [wisdom] is a tree of life to those who lay hold of her; those who hold her fast are called happy."

Thursday 4

Philippians 2:5-11

[See Thursday 2 for more on Philippians.]
Paul has been encouraging unity in the Philippians' faith: "be of the same mind, having the same love, being in full accord and of one mind" (2:2). He has also counseled them toward humility in their relationships with one another (2:3-4). In order to provide an example and encouragement, Paul quotes the lines of a hymn from the ancient church (vv. 6-11). Christ is the model for selfless service: though "in the form of God," he

"emptied himself, taking the form of a slave" (vv. 6-7). His service and obedience to God went even to the point of death on the cross (v. 8). But he is glorified by God—and by all creation—not in spite of his service on the cross but precisely because of it (vv. 9-11).

Paul implies that the path of Christian discipleship is the way of Christ's cross and resurrection: self-giving love, service, and sacrifice in order to bring to birth a new and more abundant life for others—"to the glory of God the Father" (v. 11).

Psalm 37:1-6

Carroll Stuhlmueller writes: "This poem is not so much instruction or proof as quiet meditation. Nor is it mysticism for saints—it centers on earthly problems, temptations, and occasional lapses."[15] The earthly problems seem to focus on the apparent success of ungodly, greedy, and even violent people; the temptation is to lose faith in God and God's justice.

The psalmist calls on believers not to "be provoked by evildoers" or "envy those who do wrong" (v. 1). The vocation of God's people is simple: "trust in the LORD" in their hearts and minds and "do good" in their actions. When we trust in God we believe that God acts on our behalf. We live confidently, believing that our personal integrity, the integrity of our relationship with God, and the justice of God that we long for will eventually "shine" like the sun at noon.

Friday 4

Jeremiah 12:4

We return to Jeremiah 12. The passage we examined earlier (12:10-13; see Friday, Week One) is an excerpt from God's lament; in today's verse the prophet himself speaks. He cries to the Lord, "How long will the land mourn, and the grass of every field wither?" Jeremiah appeals for God's intervention on behalf of the land and its suffering, nonhuman inhabitants (the animals and the birds).

The problem is not the land itself, for it is a good land (see 12:2; also 2:7, 21). "The land is not the problem," says Fretheim; "the issue is the people who live on it."[16] The "wickedness" of the people in forsaking the Lord has led to corruption, greed, and economic disparity. All these factors have a devastating effect on the health on the nonhuman environment. "Modern understandings of the interrelatedness of the ecosystem," Fretheim writes, "connect well with these biblical insights."[17]

Romans 8:18-25

[See Monday 2 for more on Romans.]

Not only humans but all creation longs for redemption—so writes Paul in these verses. He uses the metaphor of giving birth (v. 22) to describe the "groaning" of creation—an image that combines suffering and hope. "Creation waits with eager longing for the revealing of the children of God" (v. 19). Why?

The "children of God" are those who have been restored or redeemed in Christ ("the new Adam," 5:12 ff) to their original vocation of "serving and keeping" the garden of creation (Gen. 2:15), rather than destroying it. Those who receive the "abundance of [God's] grace," according to Paul, will exercise dominion in life rather than a sinful dominion in death. Those who are set free by Christ from the bondage of sin will participate in God's liberation of a suffering creation.

Saturday 4

Isaiah 43:15, 18-21

We return to Second Isaiah (chaps. 40–55) and to the setting of the Babylonian captivity of the people of Judah (c. 586–539 BCE). Through the prophet, God announces a "new thing" that God is about to do (v. 19). It will be a new "exodus," so to speak—an act of divine power comparable to the first exodus from slavery in Egypt: God will rescue the exiles and bring the them home to Judah.

This time, however, rather than crossing through an arid desert like their ancestors, these exiles will cross a wilderness that "springs forth" with water and life. Even the wild animals along the way will be praising God (v. 20). The promise is *resurrection*, to use a term ordinarily reserved for the New Testament. The people whom God has "formed" for God's own purposes—now in bondage—will be set free and recreated as a nation of praise rather than lament. In the prophetic view of a fully interrelated creation, the nonhuman creation will flourish as well.

Revelation 21:1-5

David E. Aune writes that, "Revelation is the book in the [New Testament] that modern Western readers find the most foreign."[18] This is probably due in large part to the fact that Revelation is an "apocalyptic" book— that is, literature that purports to reveal "heavenly secrets" (including information about the end of the world or the ultimate fulfillment of God's purposes). Apocalyptic literature both in the ancient world and in the Bible is highly symbolic, often drawing upon archaic references to "conflict and victory, suffering and vindication."[19]

Revelation was probably written by a Jewish Christian (who identifies himself as John) toward the end of the first century CE. He writes to seven churches in western Asia Minor and offers comfort, encouragement, and even reprimand (to some) as they struggle to maintain their faith and communities in the face of external persecution or internal impurity.

Our reading for tonight is from John's vision of a "new Jerusalem" when God finally makes "all things new" (v. 5). John appears to be echoing earlier words from Isaiah 65:17 ("For I am about to create new heavens and a new earth") and 66:22 ("For as the new heavens and the new earth, which I will make . . . "). An old word (Isaiah) from the Lord becomes a new word (Revelation)—and an old heaven and earth become new. Missing from the new creation will be the suffering, pain, death, and grief of the old creation.

Sunday 4

Psalm 96

This psalm proclaims and celebrates the reign of God over all the earth. It is structured with two summons to praise (vv. 1-3, vv. 7-9); motivations or contents for praise (vv. 4-6, vv. 10-13) follow each summons. Scholars generally believe that Psalms 96–99 were used within the context of worship in the Temple and that their references to the "coming of the LORD" were related to the enacting of liturgy.

Verses 11-12 summon all earth and heaven to praise, including the sea and sea creatures, fields and beasts, and the trees of the forest. In the view of the psalm, the nonhuman creation has as much reason and role as humans in praising the triumph of God's justice.

Psalm 150

Our four-week cycle of prayer comes to a close with this psalm, which seems fitting, given that Psalm 150 also brings to a close the book of Psalms. And what a closing it is! Over thirteen times in only six verses, the psalm uses the Hebrew word "hallelujah" or its derivatives (translated as "praise the LORD" or "praise God").

As James L. Mays points out, the psalm tells us *whom* to praise (v. 1, "God"), *why* God is to be praised (v. 2, God's "powerful acts" and "many great deeds"), *how* God is to be praised (vv. 3-5, with dance and musical instruments), and *who* or *what* is to praise God (v. 6, "everything that has breath").[20]

An ecological reading or singing of this psalm would hear in the phrase "everything that has breath" an inclusive summons to all life—for everything that lives *breathes*. Human, insect, bird, mammal, fish, plant, tree, bacteria—all participate in the give and take of carbon and oxygen. As in Psalm 96, everything that lives has a reason and a role in praising the God of creation.

1. Walter Brueggemann, "The Prophetical Books," in *The New Oxford Annotated Bible* (New York: Oxford University Press, 1991), 863 OT.
2. R. B. Y. Scott, "Ecclesiastes," in *The New Oxford Annotated Bible*, 841 OT.
3. Walter Brueggemann, *Reverberations of Faith: A Theological Handbook of Old Testament Themes* (Louisville, KY: Westminster John Knox Press, 2002), 106.
4. Terence E. Fretheim, *God and World in the Old Testament: A Relational Theology of Creation* (Nashville, TN: Abingdon Press, 2005), 158.
5. Ibid., 258.
6. Roland E. Murphy, *The Song of Songs: A Commentary on the Book of Canticles or the Song of Songs* (Minneapolis, MN: Augsburg Fortress Press, 1990), 97.
7. H. Paul Santmire, "Partnership with Nature According to the Scriptures: Beyond the Theology of Stewardship," *Christian Scholar's Review* 32, no.4 (2003): 394.
8. Carroll Stuhlmueller, "Psalms," in James L. Mays, ed., *Harper's Bible Commentary* (San Francisco: Harper & Row, Publishers, 1988), 444.
9. Roland E. Murphy, *The Tree of Life: An Exploration of Biblical Wisdom Literature*, 2nd ed. (Grand Rapids, MI: William B. Eerdmans Publishing Company, 1996), 84.
10. Fretheim, *God and World in the Old Testament*, 146.
11. James M. Efird, *The Old Testament Writings: History, Literature, and Interpretation* (Atlanta, GA: John Knox Press, 1982), 157.
12. Bruce Metzger, introduction to "The Letter of Paul to the Colossians," in *The New Oxford Annotated Bible*, 285 NT.
13. Efird, *The Old Testament Writings*, 53.
14. James Luther Mays, *Psalms* (Louisville, KY: John Knox Press, 1994), 220.
15. Stuhlmueller, *Harper's Bible Commentary*, 450.
16. Fretheim, *God and World in the Old Testament*, 175.
17. Ibid., 173.
18. David E. Aune, "Revelation" in *Harper's Bible Commentary*, 1301.
19. Ibid.
20. Mays, *Psalms*, 450.

SOURCES

Translations of scripture are noted below using the following:

BARNETT Thomas Barnett, trans. *Songs for the Holy One.* Kelowna, British Columbia: Wood Lake Books, 2004.

GNT Good News Translation

GRAIL *The Psalms: An Inclusive Language Version Based on the Grail Translation from the Hebrew.* Chicago: GIA Publications, 1986.

ILP *Inclusive-Language Psalms from Inclusive-Language Lectionaries for Years A, B, and C.* New York: Pilgrim Press, 1987.

NAB New American Bible

NJB New Jerusalem Bible

NRSV New Revised Standard Version

REB Revised English Bible

MESSAGE *The Message* by Eugene H. Peterson

Prayers, blessings, or translations of scripture designated SHP are by Sam Hamilton-Poore.

Musical settings for various hymns are noted below using the following:

ELW *Evangelical Lutheran Worship.* Minneapolis: Augsburg Fortress, 2006.

Gather *Gather—Second Edition.* Chicago: GIA Publications, 1994.

LMGM *Lead Me, Guide Me: The African American Catholic Hymnal.* Chicago: GIA Publications, 1987.

NCH *The New Century Hymnal.* Cleveland, OH: Pilgrim Press, 1995.

PH *The Presbyterian Hymnal: Hymns, Psalms, and Spiritual Songs.* Louisville, KY: Westminster/John Knox Press, 1990.

UMH *The United Methodist Hymnal.* Nashville, TN: United Methodist Publishing House, 1989.

WLP *Wonder, Love, and Praise: A Supplement to The Hymnal 1982.* New York: Church Publishing, 1997.

W&R *Worship and Rejoice.* Carol Stream, IL: Hope Publishing Co., 2001.

WOV *With One Voice: A Lutheran Resource for Worship.* Minneapolis: Augsburg Fortress, 1995.

The following sources have supplied more than one quotation. These will afterward be cited only by author/editor, title, and page number:

The Anglican Church in Aotearoa, New Zealand and Polynesia. *A New Zealand Prayer Book: He Karakia Mihinare o Aotearoa.* San Francisco: HarperSanFrancisco, 1997.

Bachleda, F. Lynne. *Blue Mountain: A Spiritual Anthology Celebrating the Earth.* Birmingham, AL: Menasha Ridge Press, 2000.

Belopopsky, Alexander and Dimitri Oikonomou, eds. *SYNDESMOS Orthodoxy and Ecology Resource Book.* Bialystok, Poland: Orthdruk Orthodox Printing House, 1996.

Boff, Leonardo. *Ecology and Liberation: A New Paradigm*, trans. John Cumming. Maryknoll, NY: Orbis Books, 1995.

Calvin, John. *Heart Aflame: Daily Readings from Calvin on the Psalms*. Phillipsburg, NJ: P&R Publishing, 1999.

Duncan, Geoffrey, comp. and ed. *Dare to Dream: A Prayer and Worship Anthology from Around the World*. London: HarperCollins, Fount, 1995.

Habel, Norman C. *Seven Songs of Creation: Liturgies for Celebrating and Healing Earth*. Cleveland, OH: Pilgrim Press, 2004.

Iona Community. *Iona Abbey Worship Book*. Glasgow: Wild Goose Publications, 2001.

_____. *The Pattern of Our Days: Worship in the Celtic Tradition from the Iona Community*. Edited by Kathy Galloway. New York: Paulist Press, 1996.

Kwatera, Michael. *Praise God with All Creation: A Book of Prayer for Morning and Evening*. San Jose, CA: Resource Publications, 2000.

Linzey, Andrew. *Animal Rites: Liturgies of Animal Care*. Cleveland, OH: Pilgrim Press, 1999.

Linzey, Andrew, and Tom Regan, eds. *Love the Animals: Meditations and Prayers*. New York: Crossroad Publishing Co., 1989.

McFague, Sallie. *Life Abundant: Rethinking Theology and Economy for a Planet in Peril*. Minneapolis: Fortress Press, 2001.

McGill, Daniel J. *Forty Nights: Creation Centered Night Prayer*. New York: Paulist Press, 1993.

Millar, Peter W. *An Iona Prayer Book*. Norwich, England: Canterbury Press, 1998.

Morley, Janet. *All Desires Known*. Expanded ed. Harrisburg, PA: Morehouse Publishing, 1992.

_____, ed. *Bread of Tomorrow: Prayers for the Church Year*. Maryknoll, NY: Orbis Books, 1992.

The Office of the General Assembly, Presbyterian Church (U.S.A.). *Restoring Creation for Ecology and Justice*. Louisville, KY: Office of the General Assembly, 1990.

Roberts, Elizabeth, and Elias Amidon, eds. *Life Prayers: From Around the World, 365 Prayers, Blessings, and Affirmations to Celebrate the Human Journey*. San Francisco: HarperSanFrancisco, 1996.

Rowthorn, Anne. *Earth and All the Stars: Reconnecting with Nature through Hymns, Stories, Poems, and Prayers from the World's Great Religions and Cultures*. Edited by Gina Misiroglu and Katharine Farnam Conolly. Novato, CA: New World Library, 2000.

Simpson, Ray. *A Holy Island Prayer Book: Morning, Midday and Evening Prayer*. Harrisburg, PA: Morehouse Publishing, 2003.

World Council of Churches. *Signs of the Spirit: Official Report, WCC Seventh Assembly*, ed. Michael Kinnamon. Grand Rapids, MI: William B. Eerdmans, 1991.

Wyles, Kate, comp. and ed. *From Shore to Shore: Liturgies, Litanies and Prayers from Around the World*. London: Society for Promoting Christian Knowledge, 2003.

WEEK ONE

Monday 1

Opening: Joseph Renville, "Many and Great, O God" (Public Domain); ELW 837, Gather 338, NCH 3, PH 271, UMH 148, W&R 26, WOV 794.

Hymn:	Eleanor Farjeon, "Morning Has Broken"; Gather 546, ELW 556, PH 469, UMH 145, W&R 35.
Scripture:	NRSV
Another Voice:	Augustine, *Writings of Saint Augustine*, vol. 7, *The City of God* (New York: Fathers of the Church, 1952), 219.
Prayer:	*A New Zealand Prayer Book*, 569.
Blessing:	SHP
Midday Reflection:	Wendell Berry, *What Are People For?* (New York: North Point Press, 1990), 98.
Midday Prayer:	SHP
Opening:	Ruth Burgess, quoted in Iona Community, *The Pattern of Our Days*, 91.
Scripture:	NRSV
Another Voice:	"Word Made Flesh," in *The Collected Poems of Kathleen Raine* (Washington, D.C.: Counterpoint, 2001), 45.
Prayer:	SHP
Blessing:	SHP

Tuesday 1

Opening:	NAB
Hymn:	Jaroslav J. Vajda, "God of the Sparrow"; ELW 740, NCH 32, PH 272, UMH 122, W&R 29.
Scripture:	GRAIL
Another Voice:	Ruth Page, *God and the Web of Creation* (London: SCM Press, 1996), 152–53.
Prayer:	*A New Zealand Prayer Book*, 163.
Blessing:	SHP
Midday Reflection:	"The Other," in *R. S. Thomas*, ed. Anthony Thwaite (London: J. M. Dent, 1996), 109.
Midday Prayer:	SHP
Opening:	NRSV
Scripture:	NRSV
Another Voice:	McFague, *Life Abundant*, 136–37.
Prayer:	Linzey, *Animal Rites*, 29.
Blessing:	J. Philip Newell, *Celtic Prayers from Iona* (New York: Paulist Press, 1997), 33.

Wednesday 1

Opening:	NRSV
Hymn:	Folliot Sandford Pierpoint, "For the Beauty of the Earth" (Public Domain); ELW 879, NCH 28, PH 473, UMH 92, W&R 40.
Scripture:	NAB
Another Voice:	T*he Homilies of S. John Chrysostom, Archbishop of Constantinople, on the Statues, or to the People of Antioch* (Oxford: John Henry Parker, 1842), 162.
Prayer:	Iona Community, *The Pattern of Our Days*, 117.
Blessing:	SHP

Midday Reflection: *Selected Poems and Letters of Emily Dickinson*, ed. Robert N. Linscott
                    (Garden City, NY: Doubleday Anchor Books, 1959), 54–55.
Midday Prayer: SHP
Opening: Patricia Preece, quoted in Duncan, *Dare to Dream*, 40.
Scripture: NRSV
Another Voice: Calvin, *Heart Aflame*, Day 57.
Prayer: Kwatera, *Praise God with All Creation*, 34.
Blessing: Habel, *Seven Songs of Creation*, 71.

Thursday 1

Opening: NRSV
Hymn: Edwin Hatch, "Breathe on Me, Breath of God" (Public Domain);
                    NCH 292, PH 316, UMH 420, W&R 461.
Scripture   NRSV
Other Voices: Presbyterian Church (U.S.A.), *Restoring Creation for Ecology and
                    Justice*, 19–20; Sallie McFague, *Super, Natural Christians: How We
                    Should Love Nature* (Minneapolis: Fortress Press, 1997), 166.
Prayer: The Evangelical Reformed Churches in German-speaking
                    Switzerland, quoted in Diane Karay Tripp, comp. and ed., *Prayers
                    from the Reformed Tradition: In the Company of a Great Cloud of
                    Witnesses* (Louisville, KY: Witherspoon Press, 2001), 119.
Blessing: Simpson, *A Holy Island Prayer Book*, 35.
Midday Reflection: Loren Eiseley, "The Star Thrower," in *The Unexpected Universe*,
                    quoted in Bachleda, *Blue Mountain*, 151–52.
Midday Prayer: SHP
Opening: Charles Wesley, "Come, Holy Ghost, Our Hearts Inspire" (Public
                    Domain); UMH 603.
Scripture: Mary Phil Korsak, *At the Start: Genesis Made New, A Translation of
                    the Hebrew Text* (New York: Doubleday, 1993), 5–6.
Another Voice: World Council of Churches, *Signs of the Spirit*, 55.
Prayer: Royal Society for the Prevention of Cruelty to Animals, from the
                    RSPCA Order of Service, quoted in Linzey and Regan, *Love the
                    Animals*, 58.
Blessing: SHP

Friday 1

Opening: Lutheran World Federation, quoted in Habel, *Seven Songs of
                    Creation*, 131.
Hymn: Horatius Bonar, "Come, Lord, and Tarry Not" (Public Domain). Tune:
                    St. Bride, quoted in Howard L. Rice and Lamar Williamson Jr., eds.,
                    A Book of Reformed Prayers (Louisville, KY: Westminster John Knox
                    Press, 1998), 83.
Scripture: NRSV
Another Voice: John Chryssavgis, ed., *Cosmic Grace, Humble Prayer: The Ecological
                    Vision of the Green Patriarch Bartholomew I* (Grand Rapids, MI:
                    William B. Eerdmans Publishing Company, 2003), 306.

Prayer:	U.N. Environmental Sabbath, quoted in Roberts and Amidon, *Life Prayers*, 112.
Blessing:	Millar, *An Iona Prayer Book*, 32.
Midday Reflection:	Denise Levertov, "Tragic Error," in *The Life Around Us: Selected Poems on Nature* (New York: New Directions Books, 1997), 12.
Midday Prayer:	SHP
Opening:	NRSV
Scripture:	ILP
Another Voice:	Boff, *Ecology and Liberation*, 18.
Prayer:	Stephen Orchard, "Waste," quoted in Duncan, *Dare to Dream*, 19.
Blessing:	SHP

Saturday 1

Opening:	NRSV
Hymn:	German Hymn, "When Morning Gilds the Skies," trans. Edward Caswall (Public Domain); ELW 853, NCH 86, PH 487, UMH 185, W&R 111.
Scripture:	BARNETT
Another Voice:	Presbyterian Church (U.S.A.), *Restoring Creation for Ecology and Justice*, 19.
Prayer:	SHP
Blessing:	Morley, *All Desires Known*, 88.
Midday Reflection & Prayer:	E. E. Cummings, "i thank You God," in *Complete Poems: 1904–1962*, rev. ed., ed. George J. Firmage (New York: Liveright, 1991), 663.
Opening:	Julia Esquivel V., *Secrets of God's Reign: Poems by Julia Esquivel V.*, trans. Kathy Ogle, Cecilia M. Corcoran, and Judith Moore (Washington, DC: Ecumenical Program on Central America and the Caribbean [EPICA], 2002), 61.
Scripture:	NRSV
Other Voices:	Catherine of Siena, quoted in Linzey, *Animal Rites*, 140; McFague, *Life Abundant*, 13.
Prayer:	Simpson, *A Holy Island Prayer Book*, 22–23.
Blessing: SHP	

Sunday 1

Opening:	NRSV
Hymn:	Kim Oler, quoted in Roberts and Amidon, *Life Prayers*, 383.
Scripture:	NRSV
Another Voice:	Jürgen Moltmann, *God in Creation: A New Theology of Creation and the Spirit of God* (Minneapolis: Fortress Press, 1993), 31.
Prayer:	The Brothers of Weston Priory, quoted in Rowthorn, *Earth and All the Stars*, 305–306.
Blessing:	SHP
Midday Reflection:	Galway Kinnell, "Saint Francis and the Sow," in *Three Books* (Boston, MA: Houghton Mifflin Co., Mariner, 2002), 81.

Midday Prayer:	SHP
Opening:	Kwatera, *Praise God with All Creation*, 41.
Scripture:	NAB
Another Voice:	Mother Teresa, *The Joy in Loving: A Guide to Daily Living with Mother Teresa*, comp. Jaya Chaliha and Edward Le Joly (New York: Penguin Compass, 2000), 228.
Prayer:	*A New Zealand Prayer Book*, 62.
Blessing:	SHP

WEEK TWO

Monday 2

Opening:	NRSV
Hymn:	Taiwanese Hymn, "God Created Heaven and Earth," trans. Boris and Clare Anderson; 1983 ELW 738, NCH 33, PH 290, UMH 151.
Scripture:	NRSV
Another Voice:	Martin Luther, quoted in Heinrich Bornkamm, *Luther's World of Thought*, trans. Martin H. Bertram (Saint Louis, MO: Concordia Publishing House, 1958), 189.
Prayer:	Uniting Church in Australia, quoted in Duncan, *Dare to Dream*, 16.
Blessing:	SHP
Midday Reflection:	Annie Dillard, *Pilgrim at Tinker Creek* (New York: Harper's Magazine Press, 1974), 136–37.
Midday Prayer:	SHP
Opening:	Geoff Lowson, quoted in Wyles, *From Shore to Shore*, 55.
Scripture:	NRSV
Another Voice:	Barbara Wood, quoted in Duncan, *Dare to Dream*, 6–7.
Prayer:	*Saint Gregory Nazianzen: Selected Poems*, trans. John McGuckin (Oxford: Sisters of the Love of God Press, 1986), 7.
Blessing:	SHP

Tuesday 2

Opening:	SHP
Hymn:	Isaac Watts, "I Sing the Mighty Power of God" (Public Domain); NCH 12, PH 288, UMH 152, W&R 31.
Scripture:	NRSV
Other Voices:	Catholic Bishops of the Pacific Northwest, "The Columbia River Watershed: Caring for Creation and the Common Good, An International Pastoral Letter by the Catholic Bishops of the Region" [http://www.columbiariver.org]; Samuel Rayan, "The Earth Is the Lord's," in David G. Hallman, ed., *Ecotheology: Voices from South and North* (Maryknoll, NY: Orbis Books, 1994), 132–33.
Prayer:	SHP
Blessing:	SHP
Midday Reflection:	Henry David Thoreau, journal entry for September 7, 1851, in *The Heart of Thoreau's Journals*, 2nd ed., ed. Odell Shepard (Mineola, NY: Dover Publications, 1961), 58.

Midday Prayer:	SHP
Opening:	NAB
Scripture:	NRSV
Another Voice:	*Meditations with Julian of Norwich*, introduction and versions by Brendan Doyle (Santa Fe, NM: Bear and Co., 1983), 24–25.
Prayer:	Simpson, *A Holy Island Prayer Book*, 43.
Blessing:	McGill, *Forty Nights*, 232–33.

Wednesday 2

Opening:	BARNETT
Hymn:	Cecil Frances Alexander, "All Things Bright and Beautiful" (Public Domain); NCH 31, PH 267, UMH 147, W&R 30, WOV 767.
Scripture:	GNT
Other Voices:	*New Poems by Christina Rossetti Hitherto Unpublished or Uncollected*, ed. William Michael Rossetti (New York: Macmillan and Co., 1896), 64; Thomas à Kempis, *The Imitation of Christ*, trans. Leo Sherley-Price (New York: Penguin Books, 1952), 72.
Prayer:	Gail A. Ricciuti, quoted in Rosemary Catalano Mitchell and Gail Anderson Ricciuti, *Birthings and Blessings: Liberating Worship Services for the Inclusive Church* (New York: Crossroad Publishing Co., 1991), 170.
Blessing:	SHP
Midday Reflection:	William Carlos Williams, *Collected Poems 1939–1962*, vol. 2, quoted in Berry, *What Are People For?*, 152.
Midday Prayer:	SHP
Opening:	NJB
Scripture:	NRSV
Another Voice:	Rachel Carson, *Under the Sea-Wind* (New York: Penguin Books, 2007), foreword.
Prayer:	Metropolitan Tryphon, quoted in Belopopsky and Oikonomou, *SYNDESMOS*, 23 Annex 1.
Blessing:	SHP

Thursday 2

Opening:	REB
Hymn:	Curtis Beach, "O How Glorious, Full of Wonder"; NCH 558
Scripture:	NAB
Other Voices:	Beatrice of Nazareth, quoted in Mary Ford-Grabowsky, *WomanPrayers: Prayers by Women throughout History and Around the World* (San Francisco: HarperSanFrancisco, 2003), 176; Karl Barth, *Church Dogmatics*, vol. 3, part 3, *The Doctrine of Creation*, eds. G. W. Bromiley and T. F. Torrance (Edinburgh: T. & T. Clark, 1960), 240.
Prayer:	Isidore of Seville, quoted in Rowthorn, *Earth and All the Stars*, 124.
Blessing:	SHP
Midday Reflection:	Fyodor Dostoyevsky, *The Brothers Karamazov*, trans. Constance Garnett (New York: Modern Library, 1950), 382–83.

Midday Prayer: SHP
Opening: GRAIL
Scripture: NRSV
Another Voice: *The Windows of Faith: Prayers of Holy Hildegard*, ed. Walburga Storch
                 and trans. Linda M. Maloney (Collegeville, MN: Liturgical Press,
                 1997), 65.
Prayer: SHP
Blessing: Iona Community, *Iona Abbey Worship Book*, 134.

Friday 2
Opening: *Lancelot Andrewes: The Private Prayers*, trans. David Scott (London:
                 Society for Promoting Christian Knowledge, 2002), 19.
Hymn: Fran Minkoff, "Healing River"; Gather 408.
Scripture: NRSV
Other Voices: Ronald A. Simkins, *Creator and Creation: Nature in the Worldview of
                 Ancient Israel* (Peabody, MA: Hendrickson Publishers, 1994), 6; Kate
                 Compston, quoted in Duncan, *Dare to Dream*, 22.
Prayer: Iona Community, *Iona Abbey Worship Book*, 139.
Blessing: Habel, *Seven Songs of Creation*, 200.
Midday Reflection: David W. Orr, *Earth in Mind: On Education, Environment, and the
                 Human Prospect* (Washington, D.C.: Island Press, 1994), 50.
Midday Prayer: SHP
Opening: McGill, *Forty Nights*, 59.
Scripture: MESSAGE
Another Voice: World Council of Churches, *Signs of the Spirit*, 56.
Prayer: *A New Zealand Prayer Book*, 459.
Blessing: SHP

Saturday 2
Opening: SHP
Hymn: Charles Wesley, "Christ, Whose Glory Fills the Skies" (Public
                 Domain); ELW 553, PH 462, UMH 173, W&R 91.
Scripture: NRSV
Other Voices: McFague, *Life Abundant*, 9; Marga Bührig, "What Can I Do?," in D.
                 Preman Niles, *Resisting the Threats to Life: Covenanting for Justice,
                 Peace and the Integrity of Creation*, Risk Book Series (Geneva: World
                 Council of Churches Publications, 1989), n.p.
Prayer: Jürgen Moltmann, *The Source of Life: The Holy Spirit and the Theology
                 of Life*, trans. Margaret Kohl (Minneapolis: Fortress Press, 1997), 145.
Blessing: SHP
Midday Reflection: Rainer Maria Rilke, *Rilke's Book of Hours: Love Poems to God*, trans. Anita
                 Barrows and Joanna Macy (New York: Riverhead Books, 1997), 121.
Midday Prayer: SHP
Opening: NAB
Scripture: NRSV
Another Voice: U.N. Environmental Sabbath Program, quoted in Roberts and
                 Amidon, *Earth Prayers*, 94.

Prayer: Rowthorn, *Earth and All the Stars*, 293–94.
Blessing: SHP

Sunday 2
Opening: NRSV
Hymn: Johann Mentzer, "Oh, That I Had a Thousand Voices"; ELW 833,
                  PH 475.
Scripture: "Psalm 148," in Nancy Schreck and Maureen Leach, *Psalms Anew: In
                  Inclusive Language* (Winona, MN: Saint Mary's Press, 1986).
Another Voice: Euros Bowen, "Yr Holl Fyd Sy'n Llawn Gogoniant," quoted in
                  Anthony Duncan, comp., *A Little Book of Celtic Prayer: A Daily
                  Companion and Guide* (London: Marshall Pickering, Harper Collins,
                  1996), 23.
Prayer: Anon. Welsh, "Glorious Lord," quoted in Oliver Davies and Fiona
                  Bowie, eds., *Celtic Christian Spirituality: An Anthology of Medieval
                  and Modern Sources* (New York: Continuum, 1997), 28.
Blessing: SHP
Midday Reflection: Iris Murdoch, quoted in Bachleda, *Blue Mountain*, 51.
Midday Prayer: SHP
Opening: SHP
Scripture: NRSV
Another Voice: Gertrud the Great of Helfta, *Spiritual Exercises*, trans. Gertrud Jaron
                  Lewis and Jack Lewis (Kalamazoo, MI: Cistercian Publications,
                  1989), 90–91.
Prayer & Blessing: SHP

WEEK THREE

Monday 3
Opening: SHP
Hymn: African-American Spiritual, "This Little Light of Mine" (Public Domain);
                  ELW 677, Gather 358, LMGM 190, NCH 524/525, UMH 585.
Scripture: NRSV
Another Voice: Francis of Assisi, "Wring Out My Clothes," in Daniel Ladinsky, trans.,
                  Love Poems from God: Twelve Sacred Voices from the East and West
                  (New York: Penguin Compass, 2002), 48.
Prayer: Matins Prayer, Armenian Sunrise Office, in *Let Us Pray to the Lord: A
                  Collection of Prayers from the Eastern and Oriental Orthodox
                  Traditions*, ed. Georges Lemopoulos (Geneva: World Council of
                  Churches Publications, 1996), 36.
Blessing: SHP
Midday Reflection: James B. Irwin with William A. Emerson Jr., *To Rule the Night: The
                  Discovery Voyage of Astronaut Jim Irwin* (Nashville, TN: Holman Bible
                  Publishers, 1982), 17, 60.
Midday Prayer: SHP
Opening: SHP

Scripture:	NRSV
Another Voice:	Iona Community, *Iona Abbey Worship Book*, 110.
Prayer:	Office of Worship for the Presbyterian Church (U.S.A.) and the Cumberland Presbyterian Church, *Daily Prayer: The Worship of God: Supplemental Liturgical Resource 5* (Philadelphia, PA: Westminster Press, 1987), 78.
Blessing:	SHP

Tuesday 3

Opening:	NAB
Hymn:	Thomas Obediah Chisholm, "Great Is Thy Faithfulness"; ELW 733, LMGM 242, NCH 423, PH 276, UMH 140, W&R 72, WOV 771.
Scripture:	NRSV
Another Voice:	*Catherine of Siena: The Dialogue*, trans. Suzanne Noffke (New York: Paulist Press, 1980), 290.
Prayer:	SHP
Blessing:	Edmund Banyard, quoted in Duncan, *Dare to Dream*, 4.
Midday Reflection:	Denise Levertov, *The Stream and the Sapphire: Selected Poems on Religious Themes* (New York: New Directions Books, 1997), 6.
Midday Prayer:	SHP
Opening:	NAB
Scripture:	NAB
Another Voice:	Henry David Thoreau, *The Writings of Henry David Thoreau*, vol. 5, Early Spring in Massachusetts, ed. H. G. O. Blake (Boston: Houghton Mifflin Co., 1898), March 11, 1842.
Prayer:	Metropolitan Tryphon, quoted in Belopopsky and Oikonomou, *SYNDESMOS*, 20 Annex 1.
Blessing:	SHP

Wednesday 3

Opening:	GRAIL
Hymn:	Frederick W. Faber, "There's a Wideness in God's Mercy" (Public Domain); ELW 587/588, NCH 23, PH 298, UMH 121, W&R 61.
Scripture:	NRSV
Another Voice:	Richard D. Adams, "On Fly-Fishing," in personal correspondence to SHP.
Prayer:	Attributed to Albert Schweitzer, quoted in *The Complete Book of Christian Prayer* (New York: Continuum International Publishing Group, 2000), no. 359.
Blessing:	SHP
Midday Reflection:	Holmes Rolston III, *Philosophy Gone Wild: Environmental Ethics* (Buffalo, NY: Prometheus Books, 1989), 137.
Midday Prayer:	SHP
Opening:	Lutheran World Federation, quoted in Habel, *Seven Songs of Creation*, 132.
Scripture:	NRSV

Another Voice:	Bill McKibben, *The Comforting Whirlwind: God, Job, and the Scale of Creation* (Grand Rapids, MI: William B. Eerdmans Publishing Company, 1994), 42.
Prayer & Blessing:	SHP

Thursday 3

Opening:	SHP
Hymn:	Shirley Erena Murray, "Touch the Earth Lightly"; ELW 739, NCH 569, W&R 38.
Scripture:	NRSV
Another Voice:	John Woolman, quoted in Douglas V. Steere, ed., *Quaker Spirituality: Selected Writings* (New York: Paulist Press, 1984), 165.
Prayer:	Christian Conference of Asia, quoted in Duncan, *Dare to Dream*, 9.
Blessing:	SHP
Midday Reflection:	Carl Sagan, quoted in Jeffrey Golliher and William Bryant Logan, eds., *Crisis and the Renewal of Creation: World and Church in the Age of Ecology* (New York: Continuum, 1996), 64.
Midday Prayer:	SHP
Opening:	BARNETT
Scripture:	NRSV
Other Voices:	John Chrysostom, quoted in Donald Attwater, *St John Chrysostom: Pastor and Preacher* (London: Harvill Press, 1959), 59–60; Boff, *Ecology and Liberation*, 30.
Prayer:	*The Works of Jane Austen*, vol. 6, Minor Works, ed. R. W. Chapman (New York: Oxford University Press, 1987), 456.
Blessing:	SHP

Friday 3

Opening:	BARNETT
Hymn:	Ruth Duck, "We Cannot Own the Sunlit Sky"; NCH 563.
Scripture:	NRSV
Another Voice:	Presbyterian Church in Taiwan, quoted in Duncan, *Dare to Dream*, 41.
Prayer:	U.N. Environmental Sabbath, quoted in Roberts and Amidon, *Life Prayers*, 78.
Blessing:	SHP
Midday Reflection:	Donella H. Meadows, *The Global Citizen* (Washington, D.C.: Island Press, 1991), 281–83.
Midday Prayer:	SHP
Opening:	NRSV
Scripture:	NRSV
Another Voice:	Morley, *Bread of Tomorrow*, 67.
Prayer:	Michael Counsell, comp., *2000 Years of Prayer* (Harrisburg, PA: Morehouse Publishing, 1999), 589
Blessing:	SHP

Saturday 3

Opening:	SHP
Hymn:	Johann Jacob Schutz, "Sing Praise to God, Who Reigns Above" (Public Domain) ELW 871, NCH 6, UMH 126, PH 483, W&R 56
Scripture:	NRSV
Another Voice:	Denis Edwards, *Jesus the Wisdom of God: An Ecological Theology* (Maryknoll, NY: Orbis Books, 1995), 147.
Prayer:	RSPCA Order of Service, quoted in Linzey and Regan, *Love the Animals*, 89.
Blessing:	SHP
Midday Reflection:	Philip Ball, *Life's Matrix: A Biography of Water* (New York: Farrar, Straus and Giroux, 1999), 25.
Midday Prayer:	SHP
Opening:	NRSV
Scripture:	NAB
Another Voice:	Zephania Kameeta, *Why, O Lord?: Psalms and Sermons from Namibia*, Risk Book Series (Geneva: World Council of Churches Publications, 1986), 50.
Prayer:	Linzey, *Animal Rites*, 82.
Blessing:	McGill, *Forty Nights*, 257.

Sunday 3

Opening:	NAB
Hymn:	Isaac Watts, "From All That Dwell Below the Skies" (Public Domain); NCH 27, PH 229, UMH 101.
Scripture:	NRSV
Another Voice:	Wayne Muller, *Sabbath: Finding Rest, Renewal, and Delight in Our Busy Lives* (NewYork: Bantam Books, 1999), 4–5, 6.
Prayer:	SHP
Blessing:	Early Scottish (Public Domain)
Midday Reflection:	William Blake, "Auguries of Innocence," in *The Oxford Book of English Mystical Verse*, eds. D. H. S. Nicholson and A. H. E. Lee (Oxford: Clarendon Press, 1917).
Midday Prayer:	SHP
Opening:	NRSV
Scripture:	NJB
Another Voice:	Scott Hoezee, *Remember Creation: God's World of Wonder and Delight* (Grand Rapids, MI: William B. Eerdmans Publishing Co., 1998), 52.
Prayer:	Francis of Assisi, "Canticle of Creation," quoted in Matthew Arnold, *The Works of Matthew Arnold in Fifteen Volumes*, vol. III (London: MacMillan and Co., Ltd., Smith, Elder and Company, 1903), 232–33.
Blessing:	SHP

Week Four

Monday 4

Opening:	GRAIL
Hymn:	Adelaide A. Pollard, "Have Thine Own Way, Lord" (Public Domain); UMH 382, W&R 486.
Scripture:	NRSV
Another Voice:	Calvin, *Heart Aflame*, Day 354.
Prayer:	Morley, *All Desires Known*, 23.
Blessing:	SHP
Midday Reflection:	Pattiann Rogers, *Song of the World Becoming: New and Collected Poems 1981–2001* (Minneapolis: Milkweed Editions, 2001), 69–70.
Midday Prayer:	SHP
Opening:	SHP
Scripture:	NRSV
Another Voice:	Moyra Caldecott, quoted in Rowthorn, *Earth and All the Stars*, 14–16.
Prayer:	John McQuiston II, *A Prayer Book for the Twenty-First Century* (Harrisburg, PA: Morehouse Publishing, 2004), 37–38.
Blessing:	SHP

Tuesday 4

Opening:	NAB
Hymn:	Matthias Claudius, "We Plow the Fields and Scatter" (Public Domain); ELW 680/681, PH 560.
Scripture:	NRSV
Another Voice:	*Meditations with Hildegard of Bingen*, ed. Gabriele Uhlein (Santa Fe, NM: Bear and Company, 1983), 30–31.
Prayer:	Chief Dan George and Helmut Hirnschall, *My Heart Soars* (Saanichton, British Columbia: Hancock House Publishers, 1974), n.p.
Blessing:	SHP
Midday Reflection & Prayer:	Thomas Traherne: *Selected Poems and Prose*, ed. Alan Bradford (New York: Penguin Books, 1991), 183.
Opening:	NRSV
Scripture:	NRSV
Another Voice:	Frederick Buechner, *Wishful Thinking: A Theological ABC* (New York: Harper & Row, Publishers, 1973), 18.
Prayer:	Walter Rauschenbusch, in *The Complete Book of Christian Prayer* (New York: Continuum, 2000), no. 70.
Blessing:	Simpson, *A Holy Island Prayer Book*, 34.

Wednesday 4

Opening:	Thomas Merton, *Conjectures of a Guilty Bystander* (Garden City, NY: Doubleday, 1989), 146–47.
Hymn:	Anonymous, "Christ the Apple Tree" (Public Domain); WLP 749.
Scripture:	NRSV

Another Voice: Joyce Rupp, *The Cosmic Dance: An Invitation to Experience Our Oneness* (Maryknoll, NY: Orbis Books, 2002), 67–68.

Prayer: Joy Cowley, *Aotearoa Psalms: Prayers of a New People* (Central Hawkes Bay, New Zealand: Pleroma Christian Books, 2008), no. 66.

Blessing: SHP

Midday Reflection: Barbara Kingsolver, *Small Wonder* (New York: HarperCollins, 2002), 108.

Midday Prayer: Charles Cummings, O.C.S.O.; adapted from "Fruit of the Earth, Fruit of the Vine," in Albert J. LaChance and John E. Carroll, eds., *Embracing Earth: Catholic Approaches to Ecology* (Maryknoll, NY: Orbis Books, 1994), 159.

Opening: NRSV

Scripture: NAB

Another Voice: Howard Thurman, *With Head and Heart: The Autobiography of Howard Thurman* (San Diego: Harcourt Brace Jovanovich, 1981), 8–9.

Prayer: SHP

Blessing: SHP

Thursday 4

Opening: NRSV

Hymn: Isaac Watts, "When I Survey the Wondrous Cross" (Public Domain); ELW 803, NCH 224, PH 100/101,UMH 298/299, W&R 261.

Scripture: NRSV

Another Voice: McFague, *Life Abundant*, 14.

Prayer: Wang Weifan, *Lilies of the Field: Meditations for the Church Year*, trans. and ed. Janice and Philip Wickeri (Nashville, TN: Upper Room Books, 1993), 13.

Blessing: SHP

Midday Reflection: John Muir, *A Thousand-Mile Walk to the Gulf* (San Francisco: Sierra Club Books, 1991), 77–79.

Midday Prayer: SHP

Opening: NRSV

Scripture: NAB

Other Voices: John H. Westerhoff, *Spiritual Life: The Foundation for Preaching and Teaching* (Louisville, KY: Westminster John Knox Press, 1994), 1; Ron Ferguson, quoted in Millar, *An Iona Prayer Book*, 8.

Prayer: Uniting Church in Australia, quoted in Habel, *Seven Songs of Creation*, 32–33.

Blessing: SHP

Friday 4

Opening: NRSV

Hymn: Thomas H. Troeger, "God Folds the Mountains Out of Rock"; PH 287.

Scripture: NRSV

Another Voice: Wangari Maathai, quoted in Jeffrey Mark Golliher, ed., and Taimalelagi Fagamalama Tuatagaloa-Matalavea, comp., *Healing God's Creation: The Global Anglican Congress on the Stewardship of Creation*: The Good Shepherd Retreat Center, Hartebeesport, South Africa, August 18–23, 2002 (Harrisburg, PA: Morehouse Publishing, 2004), 146.

Prayer: Christian Conference of Asia, quoted in Duncan, *Dare to Dream*, 9.

Blessing: SHP

Midday Reflection: Wendell Berry, *Sex, Economy, Freedom and Community* (New York: Pantheon Books, 1993), 32–33.

Midday Prayer: SHP

Opening: Margaret Clarkson, "Lord of the Universe," in *Psalter Hymnal* (Grand Rapids, MI: CRC Publications, 1988), no. 362.

Scripture: NRSV

Another Voice: Basil of Caesarea, *Liturgy of St. Basil*, quoted in Gordon Miller, ed., *Wisdom of the Earth: Visions of an Ecological Faith*, vol. 1, Ancient Christianity (Seattle, WA: Green Rock Press, 1997), 84.

Prayer: Rubem Alves, quoted in Morley, *Bread of Tomorrow*, 101.

Blessing: James Weldon Johnson, "Lift Every Voice and Sing" (Public Domain); ELW 841, LMGM 291, NCH 593, PH 563, UMH 519, W&R 729.

Saturday 4

Opening: NRSV

Hymn: Henry van Dyke, "Joyful, Joyful, We Adore Thee" (Public Domain); ELW 836, LMGM 197, NCH 4, PH 464, UMH 89, W&R 59.

Scripture: NRSV

Another Voice: Bede Griffiths, *The New Creation in Christ: Christian Meditation and Community*, eds. Robert Kiely and Laurence Freeman (Springfield, IL: Templegate Publishers, 1994), 80.

Prayer: *A New Zealand Prayer Book*, 181.

Blessing: SHP

Midday Reflection: "God's Grandeur," in *Poems and Prose of Gerard Manley Hopkins* (New York: Penguin Books, 1963), 27.

Midday Prayer: Iona Community, *Iona Abbey Worship Book*, 141–42.

Opening: Gregory Nazianzus, quoted in John Chryssavgis, *Beyond the Shattered Image* (Minneapolis: Light & Life Publishing, 1999), 68.

Scripture: NRSV

Another Voice: Sophie Churchill, quoted in Duncan, *Dare to Dream*, 233.

Prayer: Henry Vaughan, *SILEX SCINTILLANS: Sacred Poems and Private Ejaculations* (London: Pickering, 1847), 198.

Blessing: Adapted from Panel on Worship of the Church of Scotland, *Book of Common Order of the Church of Scotland*, 2nd ed. (Edinburgh: Saint Andrew Press, 1996), 55.

Sunday 4

Opening: SHP

Hymn: Brian Wren, "Acclaim with Jubilation," in *Piece Together Praise: A Theological Journey* (Carol Stream, IL: Hope Publishing Company, 1996), 168. Possible tune: Bereden vag for Herran (7.6.7.6.7.7. with refrain).

Scripture: "Psalm 96," in *The Saint Helena Psalter* (New York: Church Publishing, 2004), 154–55.

Another Voice:	Helder Camara, *Sister Earth: Creation, Ecology and the Spirit* (Hyde Park, NY: New City Press, 1995), 29.
Prayer:	Adapted from Thomas Ken, "Praise God, from Whom All Blessings Flow," in *The United Methodist Hymnal* (Nashville, TN: United Methodist Publishing House, 1989), no. 94.
Blessing:	SHP
Midday Reflection:	Mary Oliver, "The Summer Day," in *New and Selected Poems* (Boston: Beacon Press, 1992), 94.
Midday Prayer:	SHP
Opening:	SHP
Scripture:	BARNETT
Another Voice:	Boff, *Ecology and Liberation*, 46.
Prayer:	McGill, *Forty Nights*, 257–61.
Blessing:	SHP

The following pages constitute an extension of the copyright page.

ABOUT THE AUTHOR

SAM HAMILTON-POORE is Director of the Program in Christian Spirituality and Assistant Professor of Christian Spirituality at the San Francisco Theological Seminary. He and his wife, Terry, are ordained ministers in the Presbyterian Church (U.S.A.), and have served Presbyterian, Lutheran, and United Church of Christ congregations in North Carolina, Missouri, Kansas, Iowa, and California. Sam is also a spiritual director and frequently leads retreats related to the Christian spiritual life and the creation.

Sam was the Environmental Justice Advocate for the Presbytery of North Central Iowa and worked with the Global Warming Initiative for the Iowa Ecumenical Council of Churches. He organized and led a team of volunteers from the First Presbyterian Church of Mason City, Iowa, which monitored the water quality of a local stream. A relatively new resident of Northern California, he is enjoying the beaches, mountains, and hiking trails of the Bay Area.